Central America's Options:

Death or Life

F
1439.5
.M33
1988

Gary MacEoin

Sheed & Ward

Sheed & Ward™ is a service of National Catholic Reporter Publishing
Company, Inc.

Library of Congress Catalog Card Number: 88-60699

ISBN: 1-55612-066-4

Published by: Sheed & Ward
               115 E. Armour Blvd. P.O. Box 414292
               Kansas City, MO 64141-4292

To order, call: (800) 333-7373

Contents

Acknowledgements

Editor Tom Fox wrote in the 8 May 1987 *National Catholic Reporter:* "I asked (Gary) MacEoin in early March to go on an extended assignment for the paper. My instructions to him were straightforward: Travel through the United States and then into Central America to speak with anyone who could help update his understanding of the region's issues. Then, drawing on his background and insights, to write frankly about what he had found."

The four articles that resulted are here expanded, updated, and placed in a broader historical perspective. The scores of people who generously shared their knowledge and analyses must, for their own safety, go unnamed but not unthanked. For their professional help in reading the manuscript and providing significant substantive and editorial input I thank four committed colleagues: Peter Hinde, Diana Calafati, Betsy Cohn, and Richard Senier.

1.

El Pueblo: We the People

We have to get away from the idea that the history of America began with the European invasion of 1492, or that the history of Central America began when Christopher Columbus, on his fourth and final voyage to the Americas in 1502, landed at the Bay Islands of Honduras and sailed south along the coast to Panama.

The hemispheric population was, by the most recent estimates, about a hundred million when the Europeans arrived. That was twice the number of people then living in Europe, including Russia west of the Urals. As in Asia, Africa, and Europe, civilization developed in various centers in the Americas independently of each other, the most important being the Inca in the altiplano of southern South America, the Maya in Central America, and the Aztec in Mexico. Originally centered on the shores of Lake Petén

Itza in northern Guatemala, the Mayan culture gradually extended north into the southern states of Mexico and south into El Salvador and Honduras. Among American civilizations, the Maya were undisputed masters of abstract knowledge—writing, astronomy, calendric development, chronology, the recording of history, and mathematics. Their calendar approximated the astronomically determined year even more accurately than the Gregorian. Their mathematics, based on a vigesimal (base 20) rather than a decimal system, was an advance in knowledge that was not equalled in western Europe for many centuries. This civilization dates from the second millenium B.C., and evidence exists of human life for several thousand years earlier. The Maya numbered about ten million when the Europeans arrived.

Modern historians and geographers often include the whole of the isthmus from Mexico's southern border to Colombia under the term Central America. Here it is restricted to the five countries that have been most closely associated in recent centuries: Costa Rica, El Salvador, Guatemala, Honduras, and Nicaragua. Panama was historically part of Colombia until the early twentieth century, and Belize—long administered by Britain though always claimed by Guatemala—retains close ties to the English-speaking Caribbean.

The dominant geographic feature of Central America is the range of volcanic mountains stretching from Mexico to Panama, usually not far from the Pacific coast, with breaks in Honduras and Nicaragua permitting the construction of an inter-ocean canal. The highest peak is Tajumulco in Guatemala, an inactive volcano 13,816 feet (4.211 m.) high. The mountains divide the region ethnically as well as geographically. The highlands and the Pacific side were originally populated by Maya, later joined by Nahua from Mexico. The eastern lowlands, originally home to Chibcha, Arawak and Caribs, were later settled by African slaves imported by the British from their West Indian colonies. Population is heavily concentrated in the highlands between 3,000 and 8,000 feet. With the exception of Managua, Nicaragua, major cities are in the highlands, with Guatemala City at nearly 5,000 feet and Quetzaltenango at 7,710. The insalubrious wetlands on the Caribbean side have always been sparsely inhabited.

Most Central Americans today are mestizo or ladino, that is, of mixed indigenous, European, and African ancestry. All these countries still have ethnically unassimilated Indians (5 to 15 percent of the population except in Guatemala), with their own languages, cultural traits, and communal social structures. In Guatemala, Indians comprise between 55 and 85 percent of the population.

Spain had neither the surplus population nor the economic base to colonize efficiently the enormous territories to which it lay claim as a result of its "discoveries." In practice, it centralized its activities in the Valley of Mexico in the north and in the Andes in the south, sources of gold and silver. Central America, like other peripheral regions, was regarded mainly as a source of forced labor to be exported to other locations. More than a million were moved in the sixteenth century from the Pacific coast of Nicaragua to the mines of Peru and other parts of the empire. Many Indians also died in the frequent uprisings provoked by the rapaciousness of the colonists. Other major causes of a massive and rapid population decline included the introduction of smallpox and other epidemic diseases among nonimmunized people, starvation or malnutrition associated with the breakdown of subsistence food production, and the loss of will to live or reproduce, including infanticide, suicide and abortion. The total Indian population of the Americas fell from a hundred million to ten million between 1492 and 1560.[1]

While economically insignificant to the Spaniards, Central America was strategically important, as English and French battled with them for control of the seas and sought to capture the wealth being transshipped from Mexico and South America. It was necessary to have garrisons at critical points and to ensure that the garrisons maintained themselves to the greatest possible extent off the land. Indigo and cacao were the two first crops to be commercially exploited, and there are early accounts of Indians falling dead from exhaustion among the piles of fermenting indigo.

The agro-export system then begun was steadily expanded with the seizure of Indian communal lands. In the 1800s, coffee introduced from Africa became the principal cash crop in all Central America, followed by bananas, cotton, sugar and beef, all produced on the rich soil of the volcanic highlands, river valleys, or coastal plains. Only eroded slopes were left to the peasants to produce the corn and beans that have long been their principal food. Land concentration had become so intense by the twentieth century that a Salvadoran newspaper could write in 1928: "Now there is nothing but coffee. In the great hacienda named California that covers the flanks of the volcano Alegria,... there were formerly a hundred or more properties planted in corn, rice, beans, and fruit. Now there is nothing but coffee in the highlands and pasture in the lowlands."

Ever since the sixteenth century, residents and visitors alike have described Central America as a region of abundant fertility, a potential paradise with an excellent climate. Yet during all this period, the vast majority of its inhabitants have lived in extreme poverty and misery, while a tiny handful has monopolized wealth and power and destroyed many natural resources, such as the rain forest, by shortsighted pursuit of profit. This extreme concentration of property and wealth has been accompanied by the exclusion and marginalization of the majority of the population, thanks to the persistence of oligarchic and dictatorial political structures that historically have been impervious to popular demands. Electoral fraud is supplemented, when necessary, by death squads who assassinate democratic politicians and repress popular organizations.

Since World War II, distortion of the region's economy in favor of the agro-export sector has accelerated and the living conditions of the vast majority of the inhabitants have consequently continued to deteriorate. According to ECLA (United Nations Economic Commission for Latin America), 62 percent of the region's people live in poverty (lacking the minimum basic necessities) or in absolute poverty. Average annual per capita meat consumption by the poorer 50 percent of the population is ten pounds. The U.S. average is 175 pounds. Meanwhile, meat production for export grows, with half of the arable land now in pasture. In a 10-year period Honduran exports of meat to the United States tripled, while domestic consumption fell by 10 percent. A U.S. Department of State document in 1980 described this meat export as "a quick and dirty business" in which U.S. investors extracted the highest possible profit from converted forest land before it became eroded and worthless.

Already by the mid-1950s the social costs of this perverse form of development were affecting the urban middle sectors so severely that they began to organize to challenge the oligarchy's traditional monopolization of power and decision making. Although there has been a long history of sporadic armed revolt by the peasants, directed especially toward protecting or regaining land rights, up to the 1960s the peasants were not central actors in the anti-oligarchic coalition, which consisted principally of intellectuals, professionals, university students, elements of the urban artisan class, and state employees. More recently, their ranks have been gradually swelled by urban and rural workers until the coalition embraced what has come to be known universally as el pueblo, the people.

Only in Guatemala, however, was there a serious analysis in the 1950s of the economic base of the oligarchic power structure and a consequent challenge to the inherently exploitive nature of the primary export model. This challenge, concretized in the sweeping land reform program initiated by the Arbenz government, was beaten back in 1954 when the oligarchs with U.S. support overthrew the democratically elected government and initiated a long series of bloody dictatorships.

In the early 1960s the United States took the initiative with the Alliance for Progress to lower social tensions without changing the oppressive structures. What resulted was cosmetic and shortlived. Except for Costa Rica, the region continued to be characterized by fraudulent elections, systematic destruction of trade unions, the banning of progressive parties, killing of outspoken critics, especially journalists, violence against peasants who demanded land, and collapse of reformist programs.

Costa Rica during this period escaped the acute conflict its neighbors experienced. Its oligarchy had much stronger links with commercial capital and derived its income mainly from import-export activities, leaving it less dependent on extensive land use. Small and medium operators produced much of its coffee, and political life was more democratic and participatory. Social control has been achieved less by force than by ideological mechanisms operating through the institutions of religion and education. In spite of these differences, Costa Rica is deeply affected by the crisis of dependent capitalism. During the 1980s it has accumulated one of the heaviest per capita loads of external debt of any country in the world. U.S. subsidies—including PL 480 "Food for Peace" being supplied to 15 percent of the population—give the illusion that the problems are temporary. In fact, they are structural, as everywhere in Central America.

Elsewhere in the region, the popular frustrations had begun by the mid-1960s to incite armed insurrections. The decade of brutal repression that followed the 1954 counterrevolution in Guatemala resulted in the creation of guerrilla movements in that country between 1964 and 1966. In El Salvador, guerrilla organization began in 1973 and 1974, sparked by harsh repression and a growing conviction after the fraudulent presidential elections of 1972 that reform by constitutional means was impossible. Also in 1974 the Sandinista National Liberation Front intensified the guerrilla activities that resulted in the ousting of Nicaragua's dictator five years later.

The 1970s were marked not only by a massive growth in the anti-oligarchy movements and an expansion of their social base to include both middle sectors and rural and urban workers in coalition, but a more sophisticated analysis of the causes of Central America's malaise. The aim was no longer simply to break the oligarchy's monopoly but to change the economic system based on the export of primary products, a system now judged incapable of providing a human standard of living for all Central Americans.

Ever since the proclamation of the Monroe Doctrine in 1823, U.S. policy toward Central America has embodied a radical contradiction. It admitted in principle the sovereignty of the countries of the region but in practice exercised a veto over their choice of governments. By the middle of the last century its economic, political, and military influence had become profound and pervasive, and so it remains to this day. Regardless of which party is in power, Washington treats Central America as a zone of exclusive U.S. domination and describes it variously as "our backyard" and the fourth strategic frontier of the United States.

Only regimes approved by Washington are permitted to survive. The marines landed in Nicaragua in 1909 to prevent its president from building a canal without U.S. participation. They returned repeatedly until 1933 when they could safely leave because they had trained a National Guard headed by Anastasio Somoza Garcia to protect U.S. perceived interests. In Guatemala, as already noted, the United States ousted a president in 1954 whose reforms they judged adverse to their interests. Similarly in El Salvador in 1979 it engineered the removal of a president because it hoped thereby to head off a major threat to the status quo it supported.

Washington has always shown a predilection for the armed forces of Latin America as insurance against radical social change that would threaten U.S. interests. That was the context in which the National Guard was created by U.S. advisers in Nicaragua in the early 1930s. After World War II, the United States embarked on a program of building more professional armies, trained less to defend national borders against external aggressors than to maintain domestic order. They were to become, in effect, police forces equipped not only with military weapons but with an ideology that ensured loyalty to themselves as an institution rather than to a civilian government, and endowed with power that guaranteed them immunity from prosecution or punishment.

The rationale for the new approach was offered by General William Westmoreland at the Eighth Conference of the American Armies held in Rio de Janeiro in September 1968. He had just been named chief of staff of the U.S. Army after four years as commander in chief in Vietnam. "One only needs to read his newspaper," he told his fellow generals, "to know that the communists have used insurgent warfare throughout the world with varying degrees of success.... I feel that the prospects of repeated 'Vietnams' around the world present a very real danger to the security of every freedom-loving people. For this reason, I believe that the techniques of insurgent warfare are high on the list of threats which each of us must consider.... The propaganda describing each insurgency will picture what they term as an 'oppressed' people rising to overthrow the alleged oppressor. The objective—a communist dictatorship—will persist.... The insurgency environment is dynamic. The world has many dissatisfied people whom the communists can exploit in their quest for destruction of free society. This poses a threat that will be present for a long time."[2]

The program for training and equipping anti-insurgency forces had already been initiated five years before Westmoreland's speech. The task was assigned to the U.S. Southern Command (USSOUTHCOM) located in the Panama Canal Zone. Under this program more than 13,000 officers of the armies of Central America have been trained at the School of the Americas (Fort Gulick, Panama) in counterinsurgency techniques and pacification of civilian populations. A pastor who has interviewed many graduates of Fort Gulick in his professional work says that their personality is deformed by an intensive brainwashing which equates all protest with communist conspiracies. "There is also the brutalization that results from a regime calculated to turn a civilized person into an animal. The trainees are unprepared for a program that includes extreme brain stresses, physical stresses, emotional stresses, electric shock, and so on. An average man becomes totally unbalanced. It is very hard to get him back to a normal outlook."[3]

The Sandinista-led popular insurrection culminated in July 1979 with the ouster of the last Somoza and the formation of a government which for the first time since the Conquest was committed to respond to the needs and aspirations of a Central American people. I was one of the hundreds of journalists from many countries who went to see for ourselves. For me, long familiar with the atmosphere of fear and suspicion characteristic of those countries under oppressive dictatorships, it was an unbelievable experience. In Managua, one could walk the streets at night without fear. Nobody slunk into a dark recess at the sight of a military patrol. The children ran to welcome the teen-age guerrillas ("los muchachos") now in uniform and patrolling the streets. From all over the world came messages of congratulation and commitments to help to build the new society.

From every part of the world except from one country. All too soon it became clear that behind the grudging acknowledgments of the new regime by the United States lay a determination to prevent it from implementing its commitments to the Nicaraguan people. To accomplish that purpose the United States has since 1979 raised its intervention in the region to previously unknown heights so that it affects every aspect of the national life of every one of the five countries. U.S. policies have drawn the entire region into a conflict which in turn affects the internal processes of each country. Following decades of military rule, Honduras did seek a democratic alternative with the 1981 presidential election. Since then, however, the United States has effectively occupied Honduras militarily and made it the pillar of its Central American strategy. Honduras has, in consequence, embarked on an unprecedented process of militarization which seriously undermines its fragile democratic institutions. Human rights violations had never previously reached the systematic level characteristic of its neighbors but are occurring with increasing frequency. As the following chapters demonstrate, the short-term result is enormous suffering and loss of life. If the intervention continues, it threatens to destroy the entire social fabric and create a condition similar to that of Lebanon, a region so torn in shreds as to be ungovernable.

Notes

1. Irvin and Gorostiaga, eds., *Towards an Alternative for Central America and the Caribbean.* London: Allen and Unwin, 1985, p. 236.

2. Spanish text in *Cristianismo y Sociedad,* Montevideo, VII, 119, 1969, p. 31.

3. Personal communication to author.

2.

Survival in the Mid-1980s

As though the ravages of unending internecine strife were not enough, Central America has for several years been experiencing unprecedented and widespread drought. Clouds of dust from the parched fields swirled around our creaking, over-loaded bus as it climbed, groaning and straining, one day in March 1987 from Guatemala City toward Huehuetenango in the highlands. Some of the Indians with whom I was traveling wore distinctive garments whose intricate designs told the town or village each was from. Expressionless faces offered no clue to what they thought of the outsider.

The landscape, as we climbed to more than 5,000 feet and Lake Atitlán came in view, was indescribably beautiful. I was overwhelmed by nostalgia. For forty years I have been traveling the hemisphere from end to end, and I have seen all of this both here and in many places and countless times: the people, the now luxuriant vegetation as we near the lake, the impenetrable mountains.

Nothing seemed changed, yet I knew everything was changed. A quarter century ago, we all thought that these miniscule countries of Central America were doomed ever to suffer history, never to make it, their destiny decided by events beyond their border and their control. Today, they are caught up in a revolutionary ardor that has radically transformed the social order in one and challenges it—at varying levels of intensity—in all. It is a time of unimaginable suffering, yet a moment of intense hope. It is a good time and a good place to be alive, to be witness to, and in some small way a participant in, a dream coming to birth.

In a 1962 book I made some predictions that now return to haunt me. The title, *Latin America: the Eleventh Hour,* was apposite, although I now think that the Italian edition was more precise when it translated "Eleventh Hour" as "Ora Zero." Had I realized how close we were to midnight, I would not have confidently asserted that we in the United States had the ability and the will to fulfill the solemn commitment we made in 1961 at Punta del Este, Uruguay, in a treaty we co-signed with nineteen other American nations. That treaty, popularly known as the Alliance for Progress, pledged the signatories to dedicate the resources of the Americas to ensuring human living levels for all the peoples of the continent. I still believe we had and have the ability. I long since was forced to recognize we don't have the will.

Willie Woods, a Maryknoll priest, was one who believed we had the will and acted accordingly. I met him in Huehuetenango in 1969. He was no revolutionary. Some of his Guatemalan and U.S. colleagues thought him naive for believing he could make the system work for the Indians. He ignored his critics, and for a time events seemed to show that peaceful progress was possible. Through his organizational efforts and skills, considerable numbers of landless Indians were able to move from the highlands to new areas just then being opened for settlement near the Mexican border.

What Willie failed to understand was that the promise of land to peasants was window dressing, and that his activities were jeopardizing the real objective. A few peasant squatters made a good impression. They improved Guatemala's image, an image pockmarked by a history of shameful violation of Indian rights and sadly in need of a face-lifting. But the major homesteading project Willie envisaged threatened social upheaval. Such is the land hunger in Guatemala that the peasants would flock by the hundred thousand to any point where it was reported that land was being distributed. The Northern Transversal Strip, as the area in which Willie was working is called, has rich mineral deposits, fertile soils, and possibly as much oil as Mexico. It was intended for the army colonels on whose behalf the transnational corporations would exploit it. Indians, yes, but as landless and docile cheap labor.

One day Willie's small plane exploded not far from where I wrote these lines. In the Central American martyrology, from which with increasing frequency extracts are read when people join to celebrate Word and Eucharist, Willie's is the first name in a long list of priests, sisters, catechists, and Delegates of the Word who live in the hearts of the people. The martyrology entry for 11 November 1976 reads: "Guillermo Woods, Vietnam veteran, Maryknoll priest, missionary in Guatemala. He is a pioneer of evangelization in the Ixcán area and a promoter of cooperatives. Today we commemorate all the outsiders who have taken their stand on the side of the Latin Americans and have fallen in the struggle for justice." With him died three other U.S. citizens, lay volunteers who were part of his team. The cause of the explosion was never officially determined, though the associates and relatives of the victims were able to provide overwhelming evidence of sabotage. The Guatemalan authorities went through the motions. The U.S. State Department and the U.S. Embassy in Guatemala were as uncooperative as they were in the later and more widely publicized killing of four U.S. religious women in El Salvador. They knew in both cases that the murderers were either part of the armed forces or members of death squads working in collusion with the armed forces. Who is to say what reasons of state were more important than identifying and bringing to justice those responsible for the death of innocent U.S. citizens?

Willie's killers have since slaughtered 60,000 Guatemalans in a project that is intended to provide a final solution for Guatemala's "Indian problem." This project, which has left almost no impression on the U.S. consciousness, is one of the most important occurrences in Central America in the past quarter century. Guatemala is the only country of Central America in which the Indians still constitute a "problem." Before 1932, El Salvador's official statistics listed 20 percent of the population as Indian—not speaking Spanish at all. The massacre by the army of an estimated 30,000 in that year resulted in the abandonment by the survivors of their traditional dress and other identifying customs. The surviving Pipil, Nahua, Quiché, and Cakchiquel communities, numbered in the thousands, are marginal to the society; and this is basically true of the various Indian groups in Honduras, Nicaragua, and Costa Rica.

In Guatemala, by contrast, the majority of the more than eight million inhabitants continue to be Indian on the basis of cultural and linguistic criteria. Estimates vary from 55 to 85 percent. The Revolutionary Organization of the People in Arms, one of four political-military organizations united in a long-term struggle to end the oligarchic control of society, has summed up the situation succinctly: "According to official census reports, the Indians make up a little more than half the population of Guatemala. But applying precise cultural criteria, their numbers total, without doubt, around 70 percent of the population. The Indian map of Guatemala shows 22 different languages surviving today which are mutually incomprehensible.... Nevertheless, each of these Indian peoples considers itself to be of a common Indian heritage from the Maya nation; all have experienced the same exploitation and discrimination; all perceive themselves as poor people."[2]

The village community was always the core of Mayan society. Although under incessant attack from the sixteenth century, in the highlands it survived disease, slavery, and forced acculturation. The rise of the coffee economy in the last century posed a major threat. The government imposed obligatory labor quotas to supply the plantations, seizing so much Indian communal land as to limit the ability to grow food. Nevertheless, the Maya remained faithful to their "sacred food," the corn that has always been the basis of their economy and of central significance to their religious and cultural rites.

A remarkable revival occurred after World War II during the short democratic interlude in Guatemalan history under the presidencies of Juan José Arévalo and Jacobo Arbenz Guzmán. Between 1944 and 1950, Arévalo organized the first rural cooperatives, laid the basis for rural education, promoted Indian languages and cultures, and established local branches of political parties. The 1952 agrarian law provided an impetus to the labor movement, encouraging local and regional agrarian committees and distributing uncultivated lands to more than a hundred thousand peasant families.

The tide was reversed by the military intervention led by Carlos Castillo Armas in 1954, with thousands of peasant leaders killed or driven into exile. The Catholic church moved to fill the void, persuading the government to allow several foreign missionary orders to work in Indian communities on the understanding that their preaching would protect the peasants from "the evils of international communism." The missionaries did in fact arrive with that objective high among their priorities. As they became acquainted with the people, their problems, and their aspirations, however, many of them began to devote much of their effort to improving social and economic conditions. Large numbers of Indian youths had their first exposure to formal education, new agricultural techniques, health care, and leadership training. The missionaries encouraged cooperatives, a modern technique in tune with traditional social forms. By 1967, 145 cooperatives had a combined membership of 27,000. Less than a decade later, the number was 510 organized into eight federations with more than 132,000 members. Considerably more than half of them were in the western and central highlands, where they were having a big impact on the political attitudes, marketing strategies, and agricultural techniques of the Indians. This growth was paralleled by that of both urban and rural trade unions. The introduction of transistor radios brought a new awareness of national and international affairs.

All this progress occurred against a background of violence and struggle. After Castillo Armas seized power in 1954, thousands of kidnappings and assassinations so terrorized the people that the authorities felt confident of their ability to control. By about 1970, however, new factors came into play. The military began to penetrate northern Guatemala with development plans, placing major emphasis on the Northern Transversal Strip, where Willie Woods had for some years been opening up new land for Indians from the highlands. Simultaneously, transnational corporations appeared in the area, in search of oil, nickel, uranium, and other minerals. The government of General Carlos Arana Osorio began the institutionalization of counterinsurgency. And frustrated young people began to arm and train in the beginning of what would soon become a formidable guerrilla movement. A decade earlier some guerrilla foci had operated in the east and northeast of the country but they lacked a popular base and were quickly wiped out.

During these same years the will of the people to resist was enormously strengthened by the creation of Christian base communities. The preferential option for the poor expressed by the Latin American bishops at Medellín, Colombia, in 1968, found a ready response among the Indians. Traditionally the same leaders are responsible for civil and religious concerns, and the base communities—fed by the theology of liberation—gave direction and hope to the struggle to survive.

In February 1976, Guatemala experienced the worst earthquake in Central American history. It left 27,000 dead, 77,000 injured, a million homeless. More than 20 percent of the country's homes were destroyed. The worst damage was in the slums of Guatemala City and in the Department of Chimaltenango, where the cooperative movement was strongest. In the absence of government help, the cooperative members and slumdweller associations obtained aid directly from international organizations and began to rebuild. Simultaneously, the army began a large-scale "counterinsurgency" operation in El Quiché, the Department immediately to the north of Chimaltenango. Religious and cooperative leaders were especially targeted. Between February 1976 and the end of 1977, 40 of them were killed in Chajul, 28 in Cotzal, 32 in Nebaj, all towns in El Quiché. In the Ixcán in neighboring Huehuetenango, 68 cooperative leaders were killed. This is the area in which Willie Woods had his colonization project. His own turn had come in 1976, 20 November to be exact.

A particularly shocking massacre occurred at Panzós in Alta Verapaz in May 1978. More than a thousand Kekchi peasants marched on the town to ask the mayor about three missing peasant leaders and also about land titles the government had promised them. In the town square 150 soldiers, sent by landowners from the military base at Zacapa, opened fire and killed more than a hundred, including five children, and wounded another three hundred.

In 1980, the oppression intensified. The Catholic clerical and lay leaders, who had earlier been welcomed as bulwarks against communism, had now become special targets as being themselves communists. After several of his associates had been killed, the bishop of El Quiché, Juan Gerardi Conedera, called on all priests and sisters in July 1980 to leave the diocese. A scorched-earth policy in this and the following years brought to 60,000 the number of killed. Nearly five hundred villages were burned to the ground. Several hundred thousand Indians fled as refugees to Mexico, and another million fled south from the highlands to hide in Guatemala City slums or subsist as itinerant farm workers further south.

By this time it was clear that the Guatemalan government was using the army to carry out an enormous ethnocidal project, nothing less than to destroy the cultural and linguistic identity of the country's Indians, the majority of the inhabitants. The survivors would be organized as a cheap labor pool to serve the needs of domestic and transnational agriculture and industry. They would live in "model villages," each controlled by an army post and forming part of a "development pole."

The concept of development poles was introduced by the army in 1983 to resettle Indians displaced by the counterinsurgency war of the previous years. Six rural geographic areas were selected, the Ixil Triangle and Playa Grande in El Quiché, Yanahí in El Petén, Chisec and Senahu in Alta Verapaz, and Chacaj in Huehuetenango. They were strategically selected "areas of conflict," in which the guerrilla movement was strongest and government violence against the civilian population had been most intense. Each was to contain several strategic hamlets or model villages, to be built on the site of the former villages destroyed by the army, but designed to concentrate their population into a small area that would be easily controllable. Some 60,000 civilians now live in about 30 of these model villages.

Acul, in El Quiché, is a paradigm of this project developed with the help of U.S., Israeli, and Taiwanese advisers, utilizing the experience of the "strategic hamlets" that were an integral part of the U.S. counterinsurgency program in Vietnam, and financed in considerable part by the U.S. Agency for International Development (USAID). Guatemalan government propaganda has used it as an example of the way in which the country is being modernized, but the propaganda tells far less than half the story.

Acul in early 1983 was a village of some 4,000 inhabitants who lived in adobe houses with tiled roofs. It was well organized, with a Christian base community, development, health, education and social service committees, three schools, two community centers, and a chapel. The communal lands produced corn, beans, avocado, tomatoes and other fruits and vegetables. They had cattle, sheep, pigs, chickens, and bees. They spun and wove the wool into blankets and a wide range of useful and decorative products. Selective repression of the leaders began in 1976, and the violence became massive between 1980 and 1982. Finally, in 1983, the entire village was razed, and the survivors fled to the mountains.

Almost immediately, the army began to construct a new village and to populate it with the survivors of army raids on nearby villages, Indians captured in their hiding places in the mountains, and refugees brought from other camps. Unlike the former village, which was spread out to provide space for communal woodlands and pastures, the houses are tightly packed together to facilitate control by 150 soldiers stationed in two posts at the entrance and exit. They are made of wood with zinc roofs, building materials far less suited to the climate. The population is down to about 2,500 persons, and all the previous facilities are gone except the three schools and a health center. They no longer grow corn or any of their other foods. Instead, they produce asparagus, raspberries, brussel sprouts and Chinese pea pods for export. By mingling people of different languages and controlling production, the army achieves several objectives. The villagers cannot surreptitiously divert a share of their production to the guerrillas and friends who have escaped to the high mountains. The Indian culture is weakened by elimination of the cultivation of corn which is regarded not only as food but as religiously significant. Dependence on outside sources of basic foods creates a new level of control and facilitates the transfer of the profits of the labor of the Indians to middlemen and transnational corporations. The role of the U.S. advisers in this process is evident from a paragraph in the Santa Fe Document produced in 1980 as a policy statement on Latin America for the Republican Party, a statement that has guided U.S. policy throughout the Reagan administration. "Land, climate, and relative labor/technology costs give the United States a production cost advantage in cereal grains and beans vis-à-vis Mexico, Central America, and the Caribbean.... Small farmers in Guatemala or Nicaragua could receive greater return by converting to the production of such cash crops as asparagus, raspberries, etc., for sale to the United States, and by buying corn imported from the United States."[3]

One critical element is absent from the Santa Fe analysis. In his *Men of Maize,* Miguel Angel Asturias explains that the Maya identification with maize is so total that they think of themselves as made of maize. Then he adds what this concept means to them: "Sown to be eaten, it is the sacred sustenance of the men who were made of maize. Sown to make money, it means famine for the men who were made of maize." It is not the Indians who will get the greater return from the more rational division of labor.

Before the captured Indians are relocated in the model villages which now exist in Huehuetenango, El Quiché, and Alta Verapaz, they undergo a radical ideological reeducation in prison camps. I have talked to Indians who have been subjected to this brainwashing, and they have learned their lesson very well, if mechanically. In a toneless voice, they tell their story. They were harassed by guerrillas who tried to persuade them to join, then burned their homes and forced them into the mountains. Sometimes one will describe the attack on the village with planes and helicopters. When asked if the guerrillas have planes and helicopters, the person backs off and gives a new version omitting weaponry that only the army possesses. It is far from clear how much of this story they really believe as a result of the brainwashing. Some religious workers close to them say they have really been convinced that the guerrillas are the enemy and the army their friend. There are indications that, even if the story is at first believed, the reality slowly returns. What is evident is that they live in a state of emotional confusion and depression. Yet it is perhaps not certain that they are really confused. When talking to Indians who had fled to the mountains and later reached safety without having been captured by the army, I was told that those in the model villages do not believe a word of what they say, and that they will be the first to join the guerrillas when the opportunity offers. The army has not been able to convince people to come freely into the model villages, or to get the refugees in Mexico to return. The spirit that has held the Mayan civilization together through centuries of adversity remains unbroken.

Largely ignored by the world media, especially by the media of the United States, this revolutionary and counterrevolutionary conflict (the latter with clear ethnocidal overtones) has been more acute, savage, and prolonged in Guatemala than anywhere else in the region. Central to the conflict is the ownership of land. There is no scarcity of land anywhere in Central America. Even densely populated El Salvador has plenty of arable land to provide adequate food for all its people. The problem there, as in Guatemala and elsewhere, is that the original inhabitants have been deprived of their land by fraud and force, and the wealthy landowners keep large quantities of land idle so that the landless peasants will have to work for starvation wages in order to feed their families. Any meaningful land reform would radically undercut the unjust social and economic system. Not only would the peasants refuse to work on the traditional terms but they would begin to demand being treated as human beings. And that is what the power holders in Central America call communism.

Charging communist infiltration, the United States in 1954 supplied planes and arms to overthrow Arbenz's reform government. Arbenz's real crime was quite different. He had initiated a program to open up unused land for peasants, a program that was the first victim of his overthrow. Since that time, the subject of land reform is taboo in Guatemala. In 1983, General José Efraín Ríos Montt, the visionary disciple of the Reverend Sun Myung Moon, who had seized power in a coup, made the mistake of announcing a study of the "possibility" of land reform. Earlier he had said that if it were necessary to do away with four million Indians in order to eradicate communism, he would do that. But land reform was too high a price. Within a week of his proposal to look at it, he was overthrown. In March 1987, Marcos Vinicio Cerezo Arévalo who had been elected president in December 1985, made it clear that an elected civilian government had no intention of changing the system of landholding. Reminding his listeners in a nationally televised speech that a recent law had defined the occupation of unused land as "terrorism," he warned the peasants who had announced their intention to settle on idle lands in the hope of being allowed to cultivate them that such action would result in massacres.

Official U.S. policy supports the Guatemalan oligarchy's refusal to entertain land reform. On the same day as President Cerezo issued his warning, a spokesman for the U.S. Ambassador in Guatemala told a Witness for Peace delegation that land reform in Guatemala was "unimportant," and that there never had been a successful land reform anywhere. Guatemala's problem, he explained, is that "there are too many people in the highlands." (The spokesman might have been forgiven for his ignorance of Cuba's land reform, or the process which in the late nineteenth and early twentieth century transferred the ownership of 80 percent of the land of Ireland from absentee landlords to the tenants; but he should at least have known of the radical and highly successful land reform in Japan under the U.S. Occupation Administration after World War II).

Willie Woods' initiatives to provide land for these "too many people" were (even if he himself was less than fully aware) a reading of the signs of the times. All over Central America—as elsewhere in Latin America—el pueblo, the people, the long oppressed, voiceless, and apparently resigned masses, had begun to stir. In this sense, the U.S. Embassy spokesman was right. There are too many Indians because they have become a threat to the established disorder which it is U.S. policy to protect.

Ever since the arrival of the European invaders in America, two "subjects" have made history. One was the conqueror, the overlord, and his successors in title: Spain, England, Germany, the United States. The other was the army of occupation which mediated between the overlord and the subjugated inhabitants. Like the Herodians in Palestine in the time of Jesus or the Anglo-Indians in the Asian subcontinent, the oligarchy—continuator of the army of occupation—has mediated the orders of the overlord and until now has kept the "natives" under sufficient control to ensure a generous supply of slave or near-slave labor, ensuring the exploitation of natural resources for its own benefit and that of the overlord.

Until now. For in the past two decades the correlation of forces has altered radically. During the entire previous period, the people had been the victims of history. They had suffered it. Now they have emerged as what the Instituto Histórico Centroamericano (Central American Historical Institute), a documentation and social analysis center of the Jesuits of Central America, has named the new historic subject.

This new historic subject, to quote an Instituto study, "is an amalgam of peasants, agricultural and urban workers, rural migrants, seasonal workers and an immense unemployed population, marginated, if lucky, into informal service work. It includes the indigenous populations, blacks and mulattos, the youth, which make up more than 50 percent of the population, and women, multiply exploited by gender, race, color, and class. It encompasses the politico-military vanguards, whose project is to mobilize these groups in order to take power and put it at the service of the logic of the majorities. The concept does not exclude the unorganized masses, who are capable of insurrection at given moments and who ultimately can be incorporated into a new project. The articulated relationship of these components, when it happens, converts them into social forces and political protagonists: in other words, into a political subject that struggles for social and national liberation, sovereignty, and self-determination, and is part of an emerging project of the peoples of the third world."[4]

This active new force is opposed by the old Central American historic subject, formed by the remnants of the Creole oligarchy, the capitalist modernizers who emerged from the introduction of coffee in Central America, and the rising military, empowered by the dominant class which had reached a point where it was no longer able to maintain a submissive structure and required repression to stay in power. The arbitrator—though by no means an impartial one—in this Central American theater is the geopolitical subject, the United States. The confrontation among those subjects, opposed diametrically in their goals, values, and interests, constitutes the Central American question and challenge.

This is what is new: a people conscious of itself as a people, committed to grasp its own destiny, to build a society in which for the first time since the Conquest all will have access to food, clothing, shelter, health, education, and dignity. Modest, reasonable demands, yet demands seen not only by the oligarchy but the overlord as threatening their very existence. And in this they are correct.

South of the Rio Grande, the Europeans never completed the Conquest. Indeed, there are parts of the Guatemalan highlands in which they never succeeded in establishing an unchallenged regime, so that the people refer not to the Conquest but to the Invasion. In consequence, in Central America we have two societies and two cultures, a culture of poverty and oppression which is the only national culture, and a subculture of the external overlord which today enjoys a U.S. life style, drives in custom-armored Cadillacs, flies on monthly market runs in private planes to Miami and New Orleans, sends its children to MIT and its capital to Switzerland, enjoys the juicy pickings of U.S. subsidies, and hopes that GI-Joe will be as willing to die in Central American volcanoes as he was in Vietnam jungles to save it from communism.

In Guatemala, as in several South American countries and in Mexico, we have three cultures and indeed two civilizations. The majority of the people live by values scarcely touched by the Invasion. Thirty years ago I shared the common view that the Indians were condemned to inevitable assimilation. I no longer think so. Rigoberta Menchú's autobiography[5] is but one of myriad testimonies to a spirit that refuses to be crushed by the worst barbarities of which we are capable. It is the spirit of life which we as Christians know triumphs over death. For the Indians the Popol Vuh is the sacred book. They believe it when it tells them that "our race will never be extinguished while there is light in the morning star."

Why have the people, almost overnight, finally become a historic subject in Central America, as—in varying proportions—throughout Latin America? We have first of all the objective conditions of abject poverty and powerlessness.

To guarantee the necessary supply of low-cost labor demanded by the economic system, the vast majority of the people was from the Conquest denied access to enough land for subsistence. The late nineteenth century brought a radical change for the worse. Using their economic leverage, the industrial powers transformed the economies of Central America (as of the entire Third World) to ensure to themselves abundant cheap supplies of sugar, coffee, cotton, bananas, and beef. As earlier in England, common lands were enclosed for private benefit. Peasants and Indians were excluded from vast idle tracts, leaving them with no choice but to work for survival wages. The twentieth century has been marked by persistent deterioration of the terms of trade for the producers of primary products, due especially to technological innovation since World War II. Each year they have to sell a greater quantity of what they produce in order to buy a given quantity of the manufactures they import. Coupled with the determination and the ability of the oligarchy to maintain its living standards, this has brought a parallel decline in the share of the people. In addition, population growth—a tripling in forty years—means more mouths to share less food.

This monopolization of land ownership, carried out by "liberal" and anticlerical governments which represented themselves as taking their countries out of the obsolete ideas of the mercantilist era into the promised land of contemporary capitalism, is the key to everything that has since affected the region. By reducing the labor force's share of the benefits of the common enterprise to what was needed to ensure its reproduction, the landowners quickly accumulated capital. Some they invested in extending their coffee plantations, more in financial and commercial activities, and even more they exported to the world capital markets where it was safe from the instability of their dictatorial regimes.

Only later did they become interested in the industrial processing of their agricultural products and in crop diversification, a development that further increased their dependence on the foreign markets. Then came the Great Depression of the 1930s which hit the producers of primary products even harder than it did the industrialized countries. The price of coffee, sugar and other crops fell so low that it did not pay to harvest them. The starving peasants rose up in spontaneous land seizures which were ruthlessly suppressed by the military. In El Salvador, whose population was then two and a half million, an estimated thirty thousand were slaughtered in cold blood, another hundred thousand driven into exile in neighboring Honduras. The actual numbers will never be known, but what is important is the folk memory. "Behind every Salvadoran stand thirty thousand dead," wrote poet Leonel Rugama. *La matanza* ("the slaughter") is embedded in the subconscious of Salvadorans in the same way as the Great Hunger of the 1840s in that of the Irish. It is a barrier against every attempt at dialogue between the people and the oligarchy.

After World War II, production of coffee expanded enormously, and temporarily high prices brought good times for the region. Cotton became important after 1950, causing a further concentration of land ownership for efficient use of machinery. Sugar production rose when the United States in 1960 canceled Cuba's sugar quota. In cooperation with the transnational corporations, industries were created to produce consumer goods previously imported. Failure to correlate this import-substitute industry with the agricultural and livestock sectors of the economy, however, meant that nearly 90 percent of the industrial inputs had to be imported, while agriculture stagnated. The industrialized countries, faced with the growing cost and rapid obsolescence of technology, continually modified the terms of trade in their own favor, charging more for their products and paying less for the agricultural produce and other raw materials they purchased.

Some figures will illustrate the impact of all of this on Central America. Up to 1970, Central American economies had no significant external debt, inflation, fiscal deficit, or monetary instability. These began in the 1970s in Costa Rica, Nicaragua, and Honduras; in El Salvador and Guatemala, in the 1980s. The world recession, which began in the late 1960s and increased its intensity during the 1970s, added to other factors, such as the growing internal instability and increased investment in armaments and counterinsurgency training. Between the first quarter of 1980 and the last quarter of 1985, prices for bananas fell 26 percent on world markets; coffee prices, 23 percent; and cotton prices, 47 percent. These three commodities in 1985 accounted for 53 percent of Costa Rica's exports, 63 percent of El Salvador's, 36 percent of Guatemala's, 63 percent of Honduras's, and 51 percent of Nicaragua's.

A surplus of petrodollars in world financial markets in the 1970s allowed the Central American and other Third World countries to borrow extensively at favorable interest rates. The squeeze came in the early 1980s when interest rates jumped and many loans fell due. Unable to service their debts, most countries turned to the International Monetary Fund which insisted on austerity programs that most affected the poorer sectors of the population. Wages were frozen. Price subsidies were cut on rice, cooking oil, beans and other staples. Devaluation of currencies accelerated inflation. In Central America, the debt burden jumped from $8.5 billion in 1980 to $14.8 billion in 1984 and more than $18 billion by 1987. Costa Rica, once the model of social progress in the region, now has one of the highest per capita debts in the world.

Meanwhile, the region's economic managers, pursuing policies dictated by U.S. "advisers" of the Milton Friedman school, had achieved the world's worst income distribution. By 1986, real per capita income was down to 1972 levels in Guatemala, Honduras, and Costa Rica; to 1960 levels in El Salvador. (Because of the U.S. trade embargo and economic sabotage, Nicaragua requires separate treatment. See p. 84.) But the impact was not felt equally by all social sectors. Peasants and workers were the most acutely affected.

In El Salvador, for example, the minimum wage has remained substantially unchanged since 1978, while the purchasing power of the monetary unit is now three-tenths of what it then was. Were it not for artificial injections from the U.S. treasury, combined with the remittances to their families from undocumented Salvadorans in the United States, the disaster would be even worse. U.S. aid, which by fiscal 1988 had grown to the equivalent of $1.10 for every $1 of the Salvadoran national budget—by far the highest percentage among U.S. aid recipients—has gone almost in its entirety to keeping the government and the armed forces functioning, so that it is not helping to change the underlying conditions. The social benefit is further limited because of the Reagan administration's obsession about the benefits of private enterprise as compared with public spending. Much of the aid has gone directly to the oligarchy, with no observable trickle-down results but with an obvious relationship to the capital flight of $1 billion in the past seven years.

Ironically, it is the money sent home by Salvadorans in the United States, of whom more than 600,000 are undocumented, that keeps the country afloat and eases the social tensions. It has now replaced coffee as the principal source of foreign exchange, an estimated $1.4 billion a year, twice the national budget. A 1987 survey by an economist employed by Catholic Relief Services (U.S.) in a typical slum in San Salvador revealed a precipitous growth in the slum population since 1978, thanks to the continuing air and ground attacks on the civilian population in much of the countryside by the armed forces.

The survey established that 60 percent of these slum dwellers were unemployed, and that only 29 percent of those employed were being paid the legal minimum salary. All the others were dependent for survival primarily on remittances from refugees in the United States. Repatriation of any significant number of those refugees, as envisaged by the Simpson-Rodino legislation enacted in 1986, would have a double negative impact: loss of income to dependents in El Salvador; and a further increase in unemployment, already 50 percent nationwide. Repatriation of even one hundred thousand, according to the Human Rights Institute of the Central American (Jesuit) University, would so aggravate social unrest that it would be "the death blow of the Duarte government." Although often earning less than the legal minimum, a Salvadoran in Los Angeles makes as much in a day as a farm worker makes in El Salvador in a month; in three days, as much as a teacher in a month.

Like El Salvador, which now receives three quarters of a billion dollars from the U.S. Treasury yearly, the stagnant economies of Costa Rica and Honduras limp along on the half billion each receives. Such economic domination entails a serious loss of sovereignty in all three countries. Since much of the subsidy is in the form of loans, the external debt continues to swell. For most countries, servicing this debt absorbs 40 percent of receipts from exports.

Nor is the benefit to the region proportional to the magnitude of the subsidy. The growing recolonization produces fights within the oligarchy over the division of the spoils. Corruption extends to the banks and the USAID programs. "Free zones" are created for the benefit of the military and their suppliers. Corruption and expansion of the service sector produce a nouveau-riche class that is even less productive than the old oligarchy. Meanwhile all sectors of the oligarchy refuse to cooperate in the U.S. project designed to reduce social tensions by modernizing the system, although such modernization would objectively increase the prospects for postponing their inevitable demise. They simply live for the day. Jaime Rosenthal Oliva, vice president of Honduras, for example, told U.S. television in March 1987 that almost a third of the U.S. economic aid to his country was lost through corruption and half the remainder was used inefficiently. Several Honduran political and economic scientists confirmed this judgment for me. "The rain of dollars," they said, "is completing the disintegration of our society."

The Costa Rican crisis requires separate consideration. At first ignored because of its lack of exploitable resources, Costa Rica was settled by small farmers from Spain and by Spaniards wanted for crimes they had committed in the more organized parts of Spain's American possessions. Lacking an Indian labor force, it escaped the pattern established elsewhere of huge land holdings and land-poor masses. The banana companies established U.S. hegemony nearly a century ago, while permitting the development of liberal democratic institutions and widespread social security after World War II. Like Uruguay, however, which had a similar experience, Costa Rica's economic base collapsed in the 1970s with world recession and expensive oil, demonstrating once more that liberal reforms do not bring sustained wellbeing in peripheral countries.

Bad times have brought significant social discontent. Although the constitution in effect since 1949 forbids an institutional military, it is becoming harder to draw the distinction between the country's security forces and an army of the kind that is banned. The security forces, known as Rural Guards and Civil Guards, have more than doubled in size since 1979 to a current strength of about ten thousand. The United States provides the military and counterinsurgency training, and the weapons. Within six months of the initiation of this U.S. training program, Costa Rican security forces on the Nicaraguan border were dressed in battle fatigues and equipped with G-3 automatic weapons. There is, in addition, a civilian militia, also some 10,000 strong. Spending on police and security forces has grown more than four-fold since 1982, and since 1984 four counterinsurgency battalions have been trained.

It is, I hope, clear from all the above that today's revolutionary movements have not caused the breakdown of Central America's society and economy. That system broke down because it had ceased to be minimally functional. Nor can Washington's manipulated elections intended to create phantom democracies reverse the process. The experience of the government of José Napoleón Duarte, elected president of El Salvador for five years in May 1984, has demonstrated the inadequacy of this approach.

Duarte had been president from 1980 to 1982 of the Junta that governed El Salvador from October 1979 until the 1984 elections, and his years as Junta president were precisely those of bloodiest repression, the years in which major opposition leaders were killed or exiled in order to create a situation in which elections could be held without fear that a candidate of the people would win. After his election as president in April 1984, he was able to permit a moderate political opening, but only because the United States wanted to create the impression that the country was moving toward democracy. Meetings, mass demonstrations of workers demanding wage increases and of the unemployed demanding work, and even some political presence of the officially banned popular organizations followed his inauguration. Violations of human rights became more selective, although the number of captures, tortures and violent deaths remained unacceptably high. Nor was he able to bring to justice a single one of the right-wing leaders or army officers known to be responsible for thousands of murders. Torture of suspects to obtain confessions that are accepted as proof of terrorist activities by the courts has continued to be standard practice. The death squads remained in place, although temporarily partially restrained. And, as we shall see below, by the second half of 1987, there was a new upsurge of violations of human rights, including torture, disappearances, and killings.

Only the views of the most reactionary elements are expressed in the Salvadoran media. Nobody has dared publish an independent newspaper since 1980 when the editor and a staff member of one paper mildly critical of the regime were tortured and killed by a death squad, their mutilated bodies left on a main street of San Salvador, and bombs destroyed the offices and printing presses of another paper.

More than three years after Duarte took office the war continued, with heavy casualties, dislocation of the civilian population, and inconclusive results. The dialogue with the political leaders of the center-left and left and the leaders of the armed resistance, which Duarte promised in his election campaign and for which Archbishop Rivera Damas unceasingly calls, remains frustrated by the oligarchy, the armed forces, and the United States. To retain the pretence of power that is so dear to him, Duarte is reduced to supporting the army's "United to Reconstruct" project. This so-called "low intensity warfare" is in fact total war, with military, psychological, ideological, and political components. As Duarte's popularity, prestige, and capacity to govern fall to an all-time low, unrest grows and causes the army to increase repression and narrow the political space that had been opened with Duarte's election.

Duarte's ultimate and fatal weakness, however, is his lack of a popular base. The Christian Democrats were never more than a minority party in the center and center-right of the Salvadoran political spectrum. Christian Democracy developed in Europe after World War II less as a political ideology or philosophy than as a pragmatic centrist party to replace the discredited totalitarianisms of the right and a bulwark against the popular movements of the left that threatened the interests of big business. It never struck deep roots in Latin America, being in reality yet another form of cultural imperialism, depending for ideas and financial backing on the European parties, especially that of West Germany, and following the Germans as they moved progressively to the right. In El Salvador, the party split in 1980 over the U.S.-imposed project characterized as "reform with repression," the center joining the Democratic Revolutionary Front (FDR) in a coalition with the parties of the moderate and the far left. After the top FDR leaders were killed by a death squad while meeting openly in a Catholic high school in San Salvador, the others went into exile. Since then the majority of Salvadorans are unrepresented in the political arena, with Duarte to the right of center implementing Reaganomics and the powerful ARENA lunatic fringe on the far right sabotaging any attempt at social change. In spite of the risks involved in failing to have one's *cédula* (identification papers) stamped by the polling officials, 57 percent of Salvadorans abstained from voting in the municipal and legislative elections of 1985, a striking affirmation of protest.

The civilian presidents in Guatemala and Honduras are equally ineffective because equally powerless. Decision making remains with the military and the private sector. During his 1985 electoral campaign, Marcos Vinicio Cerezo Arévalo promised that, if elected, he would investigate all charges of atrocities by the military and punish the guilty. Immediately on taking office, he announced that there would be neither enquiries nor trials. Later he explained why he changed his mind. The military, he said, had 90 percent of the power and he had only 10 percent. During his presidency, some problems have grown worse, notably the level of personal insecurity and the cost of living. More than half the work force is unemployed, and most of those with work do not earn enough to feed their families. Yet any public mention of reforms, particularly of land reform, is immediately followed by rumors of a coup. Such a coup would make little difference, other than to end the pretence of a movement toward democracy. The army monopolizes power, and it remains committed to forcible relocation of the Indians into the "model villages" that in reality are internment camps, and to massive compulsory organization of civilian militias. It continues to use torture, "disappearances," and mass killings to the extent that the implementation of these policies requires.

The failure of President Cerezo to effect substantive change was underscored by the Health Delegation sent to Guatemala in May 1987 by two U.S.-based Health Rights organizations.[6] "It became strikingly clear to us," the study concluded, "that the repressive apparatus responsible for past massacres, scorched-earth tactics, disappearances, and assassination is still in place in Guatemala. The structures which squelched previous grassroots attempts at addressing the most basic health needs of the majority of Guatemalans, which we perceive to be potable water, nutrition, sanitation, and housing, have not changed with the Cerezo administration. It was obvious to the Delegation that the army holds the majority of the power in Guatemala. Furthermore, we saw no indication to suggest that the balance of power and its effect on the development of health care will change in the foreseeable future."

Guatemala differs from El Salvador, Honduras, and Costa Rica in one significant respect. It has kept its distance from the U.S. policy of isolating Nicaragua. This stand was formalized by President Efraín Ríos Montt in 1982, reportedly because of an understanding with the Nicaraguan government that if it did not help the Guatemalan guerrillas, he would not help its enemies. His successor, General Oscar Humberto Mejía Víctores, reaffirmed Ríos Montt's position after a short flirtation with the idea of reviving the moribund CONDECA, a U.S.-sponsored joint striking force of El Salvador, Honduras, and Guatemala "to contain Nicaraguan export of revolution." CONDECA had originally been created in 1964 to coordinate the defense forces of all five Central American countries but had effectively ceased to function after the 1969 war between Honduras and El Salvador. A major reason for Mejía Víctores's decision not to cooperate was that he, as head of the best trained army in the region and president of the biggest country, was unwilling to give the supreme command to a Salvadoran general. The United States project called for Salvadoran leadership which Washington was confident it could manipulate to pursue policies hostile to Nicaragua. The Guatemalan army, in addition, was fully extended in pursuit of the endemic guerrilla movements. It was unwilling to risk involvement in a regional war. Finally, both oligarchy and army want Mexico's goodwill and help to get back the hundreds of thousands of Guatemalan refugees, many in camps, the majority scattered near the border and in the interior of Mexico. As a major proponent of the Contadora peace initiative, Mexico opposes the military solution implicit in the revival of CONDECA.

Guatemala was able to maintain a position of relative independence from U.S. policy for two reasons. Its more buoyant economy long enabled the army to obtain weaponry from various sources. In addition, after the U.S. Congress had restricted supplies because of Guatemala's egregious violations of human rights, Israel had—with the encouragement of the U.S. administration—substituted as surrogate. More recently, however, the recession and the cost of the counterinsurgency have taken their toll. With the Reagan administration ignoring the continuing gross violations of human rights, Guatemala is once again receiving U.S. economic and military aid, and this always carries a political price tag.

In Honduras everyone marvels at Gautama Fonseca. A newspaper columnist, he says things that others only think. But, as he himself told me, he is really the palace jester whose role is to poke fun at the emperor without overstepping the bounds. The emperor is not President José Azcona Hoyo, whose role for Fonseca is that of a well paid office boy, but the U.S. ambassador who parades Fonseca's columns before visiting congressmen as proof positive of the total freedom of the media.

The extent of that freedom may perhaps be gauged by the fact that nobody in Honduras has ever read in the local press or heard on radio or TV about the Sanctuary movement in the United States or Witness for Peace or the Pledge of Resistance or the Ploughshares or any other expression of U.S. citizens' opposition to the Reagan administration's foreign or domestic policies.

Typical of Fonseca's approach was a recent column on the U.S. land, sea, and air forces which, like the air, are everywhere in his country—on the frontiers, on the beaches, in valleys, and in mountains. They have given Honduras more airfields in proportion to population than any other country in the world. They travel in packs of vehicles without license plates "because in nobody's land identifications are unneeded."

Washington pays generously for the use of this aircraft carrier strategically anchored in the heart of Central America. Ignoring congressional restrictions, the U.S. administration has built permanent installations which the Pentagon seems committed to retain indefinitely, even should Nicaragua cease to be the threat the administration claims it now is to our national security.

Corruption has long been endemic in Honduras, but the flood of dollars has raised it to new heights. Army officers are the principal beneficiaries, and they have become so powerful that the civilian government has no control over them. To win agreement from the military to hold elections in 1982, the political parties had to make a pact guaranteeing that the army would continue to have complete control over security even after a civilian administration had been installed. This pact was strengthened in 1984 when the Honduran Congress changed the Constitution so that juridically the armed forces are no longer even formally under civilian authority. The commander-in-chief, chosen and removed by the senior officers, has replaced the president as the ultimate decision maker. He in turn names the Defense Minister and the Minister of Foreign Affairs. So much for the growing democracy for which the U.S. State Department constantly takes credit.

In Honduras, the objective conditions of poverty and powerlessness are more pronounced than elsewhere in the region. Although it is the richest in natural resources of all the Central American countries, in terms of gross national product it is the poorest. The wealthiest 10 percent of the population enjoys 50 percent of the national income, while the poorest 20 percent subsists on 3 percent. In spite of these objective conditions, the emergence of the people as the new historic subject committed to assume control of its future is here less advanced than in the three countries it borders. For a time in the early seventies, it looked as if a great awakening was on the horizon. Honduras had then the most advanced labor and campesino trade unions and other organizations in the region, supported by a progressive church ministry that included encouragement of Christian base communities and radio schools. From the mid-1970s these movements were crushed by savage repression, particularly in the banana and African palm plantations along the northern coast. Today's surface calm, nevertheless, is unlikely to last long. The high level of skills and organization that result from several generations of work in the banana industry survive and can easily be translated into effective forms of resistance. The de facto occupation of the country by the United States over the past several years is bringing together a broad coalition of opposition. Honduras is catching up with its neighbors.

Notes

1. *La Sangre por el Pueblo*. Managua, Nicaragua: Instituto Histórico Centroamericano, 1983, p. 254.

2. Irvin and Gorostiaga, eds., *Towards an Alternative for Central America and the Caribbean*. London: Allen and Unwin, 1985, p. 244.

3. The Committee of Santa Fe, "A New Inter-American Policy for the Eighties," Washington, D.C., May 1980.

4. *Envío,* Jan.-Feb. 1986. Managua, Nicaragua:Instituto Histórico Centroamericano, p.1.

5. *I, Rigoberta Menchú.* London: Verso Editions/NLB, 1984. Distributed by Schocken Books, New York.

6. Guatemala Health Rights Support Project, Washington, D.C., and National Central America Health Rights Network, New York.

3.

Multiple U.S. Roles

Visiting U.S. embassies for briefings by experts of the State Department, U.S. Information Service, Foreign Commerce, USAID, and the Pentagon (military attachés) has provided me with light diversion as I have roamed Latin America for forty years. CIA operatives always wore other masks, but their disguises were not always unimpenetrable.

I have seen many changes. Embassies used to be accessible, gracious buildings, with vast expanses of glass walls, and open doors to welcome visitors. Now they are windowless fortresses, surrounded by rows of concentric walls and further out, steel and concrete cheveaux-de-frise to deter motorized kamikaze attackers.

Inside, while armed guards stand trigger ready, the visitor is X-rayed for secret weapons. Cameras are impounded. A journalist will also lose his tape recorder unless he protests vehemently. As I worked my way through labyrinthine passages on recent visits, I was reminded of the approach to the mysteries hidden in the depths of the Great Pyramid of Egypt, and I wondered if those herein enclosed are not as removed from the hostile outside reality as were the dead pharoahs in their tombs. At least, the pharoahs had the grace to leave us architecturally magnificent mausoleums.

What the briefing officers say makes one suspect that they are in fact equally removed. Like the zombies in Guatemala's model villages, who have been brainwashed with techniques developed by Taiwanese psychological-war advisers, they glibly if unconvincingly distort the reality around them, including their own role. Formerly, they spoke for quotation. For several years, however, everything is either background or deep background, the former attributable to a U.S. "official source," the latter only to "a reliable source." Ambassador Edwin Corr, in San Salvador in March 1983, gave me an hour's deep background, authorizing me to quote one short statement, which I gladly do (below). After that, I stopped going to embassy briefings, preferring to discover from my own reliable sources what transpired. Anything I attribute to Ambassador Corr other than the quote is from briefings I did not attend.

Palmerola is the heart and nerve center of the U.S. air and ground occupation forces in Honduras, Joint Task Force Bravo. There, after being cautioned not to photograph any of the dozens of radio transmission and radar towers, anything surrounded by barbed wire (as almost everything was), or any of the approaches, and not to go anywhere unaccompanied, I was informed that this is a Honduran base, U.S. personnel being present only as guests. In fact, as I learned elsewhere, Honduran soldiers are used solely to clean latrines and perform other housekeeping duties. They are not trusted even to stand guard.

The briefing room, though built to survive with minimum upkeep for a long lifetime, is classified as temporary in Pentagon-speak, Congress having prohibited the establishment of any permanent U.S. facilities in Honduras. Various kinds of seating are designated as assigned to different ranks. I was upgraded to a padded armchair reserved for 3-star generals so that I might be given the facts of life in comfort, on a background basis, by a colonel and a captain. The colonel deftly handled dozens of charts and referred frequently to a big map dotted with the scores of airstrips with which we have enriched every nook and corner of this ox-cart country, airstrips with runways and other facilities to receive and service our biggest and most advanced military aircraft. Elsewhere I learned that Honduras has more airstrips in proportion to population than any other country in the world. The colonel agreed to be photographed but not with the map. The natives, he explained, might not like to be shown all those airstrips, of whose existence—by his logic—they are unaware.

The colonel had set the scene by pointing out a long border on the other side of which the Sandinistas had built up a military machine that threatened to overrun Honduras, forcing us to come to protect them. This we do by the deterrent effect of our presence, the encouragement we give the Hondurans to resist the aggressors, the enhancement of the weapons of war we leave behind after each of the massive maneuvers that have succeeded each other without interruption since mid-1983, and the training which the Honduran armed forces receive side-by-side with our troops and airmen.

He did not explain why a nation of 2.8 million people, with more territory than it can exploit and no industrial base to support a war of aggression, its resources exhausted by the U.S. trade embargo and the sabotage of the contras, would want to take on a neighbor with a million more people and an overwhelmingly superior air force.

Nor did he show any awareness that the Honduran armed forces are concerned not about Nicaragua's intentions but those of its traditional enemy, El Salvador. For them, Nicaragua is no threat. If in a moment of lunacy or desperation it were to attack, Honduran planes could destroy its Russian helicopters and the Russian tanks unsuited to mountain warfare, knowing that its U.S. allies would block replacements. El Salvador is a different issue. The two countries have unresolved border problems, including the critical question of direct Honduran access to the Pacific. Overcrowded El Salvador desperately needs land if it is to satisfy the demands of its landless peasants without breaking up the estates of its powerful Fourteen Families. Its army, victor in a border war in 1969, has since grown from 14,000 in 1979 to 30,000, massively equipped and intensively trained by the Pentagon, with Taiwanese instructors in psychological warfare and Israelis in unconventional warfare, plus elite shock battalions trained in the United States. For the Hondurans, this is the enemy. Nor could they count on U.S. intervention in their favor in a war with El Salvador, as they could in one with Nicaragua.

The captain took over from the colonel to describe the social benefits resulting from the U.S. military presence. He waxed eloquent as he told how both the permanent garrison and the constantly changing National Guard and reservist units—currently, mostly reservists—enhance the natives' appreciation of the United States. They bring old toys and Salvation Army-supplied used clothes, pass out gum and organize social events. When troops on maneuvers don't eat all their K-rations, they carefully collect the fragments. "These the children really love."

Every medical doctor who comes to Honduras as part of an exercise makes one good-neighbor field trip to examine and prescribe for several sick peasants. Our generosity is such, the briefer stressed, that we think nothing of the $10,000 it costs to put the helicopter in the air for each of these one-day house calls.

What the doctors learn on their one-day exposure to Honduran reality is amazing. One who recently briefed visiting congressmen and other VIPs told them there is no malnutrition because everyone has land. In fact, denial of access to land underlies the fact that, by government measure, 57 percent of the economically active cannot provide the basic food basket to their families. Land concentration continues. The contras have driven thousands from the areas along the Nicaraguan border where they have built bases. In the north, United Brands has regained effective control of Las Isletas, the vast banana cooperative, with army aid to kill leaders and domesticate the trade union.

Neither of the briefings touched on issues raised in a letter signed by leading citizens of the neighboring city of Comayagua sent in March 1987 to the municipal council, with copies to the Minister of Justice, the Supreme Court, and the heads of the armed services. The creation of prostitution centers, red-light houses, and bars, it said, has brought shocking problems. The gangsters who operate these locations kidnap youths of both sexes, violate peasant women, and kill anyone who interferes. Prostitutes forced to serve a quota of clients at $2 each have been driven to suicide. A local priest who confirms these complaints adds that AIDS, previously unknown, has become a major threat.

Embassy briefings tend to be less naive and the guidelines of Administration policy are more obvious. A constant theme is that land reform is unimportant. The existence of widespread and extreme poverty is admitted, but the solution proposed is always the development of large-scale export agriculture, using mechanization and heavy input of fertilizer and pesticides as in the United States. This approach, it is argued, will so stimulate the economy that the benefits will trickle down from big business to all sectors of the community. It is easy to recognize in such discussions the underlying assumption that the peasants are poor because they are lazy and improvident.

Following the instructions of the Santa Fe Document, those sectors of the church which are putting into practice the preferential option for the poor made by Latin America's bishops at Puebla in 1979 are constantly ridiculed. Liberation theology is presented as nothing but a Marxist ideology that teaches class warfare. The fundamentalist churches which preach an individualistic spirituality without social content are described as doing an excellent job by encouraging their members to live good lives and obey their rulers. A contrast is made between their preachers and the Catholic priests. While the former live in the villages all the time and help the people, the latter come only on Sunday to say Mass and preach politics.

What Washington does not want to hear about violations of human rights it tells its representatives not to report. In Nicaragua, members of the long-term teams of Witness for Peace have for several years been going through the contra-infested areas, collecting firsthand accounts of torture and mutilation of civilians by the contras, photographing the mutilated corpses. Early in 1987, an indiscreet aide in the embassy's Human Rights Section told them to stop delivering copies of their findings to the embassy. The State Department had said that if they didn't stop cabling such data, "there would be changes in the embassy staff."

All of this might be dismissed for the nonsense it is, were it not the stuff of which U.S. policy for Central America is made, an integral part of an all-embracing plan by which Central Americans are compelled to live and, increasingly, to die.

One reason why it is important to be aware of what these U.S. spokesmen are saying is the role it plays in informing, or rather in disinforming U.S. public opinion and public understanding of the issues. Their version of the reality of Central America and of the U.S. role therein goes to a much wider audience than visiting congressmen and other VIPs. It dominates the written and electronic media in the United States. A good example of *how* manipulation of the news works is provided by the coverage in *The New York Times* of events in El Salvador during the six critical months before, during, and after the May 1984 presidential election in which José Napoleón Duarte was the winner. The *Times* is by far the most influential U.S. newspaper, providing all the news and views it sees fit to print and thereby setting the tone and often the terms of national debate. An analysis of its coverage of those six critical months reveals that 80 percent of all stories were based on information from U.S. official sources, usually White House, State, Pentagon, or Embassy, individuals who spoke "on condition they not be identified." Another 17 percent came from oligarchy or Salvadoran military sources. The people, who were the voters in what all U.S. officialdom claimed was a truly democratic exercise of the franchise, were heard from 3 percent of the time.

The day before the election the *Times* described the candidates. Duarte, who is close to Ronald Reagan and Margaret Thatcher on the far right of the political spectrum, was called a moderate leftist. Roberto D'Aubuisson, whom ex-Ambassador to El Salvador Robert White had identified as a psychotic killer and the "intellectual assassin" of Archbishop Oscar Romero, and who was named by Duarte in November 1987 as the one who ordered Romero's killing, emerged as "a hard-hitting conservative." That more than half of all Salvadorans, from center to left, had no candidate in the U.S.-controlled elections went unnoted.

The coverage of that election was extensive, if one-sided, and coverage of El Salvador for the previous several years had also been extensive. But soon afterwards, El Salvador disappeared from the news, returning only very briefly in October 1986 when the capital was devastated by an earthquake. Yet the newsworthy situation remains basically unaltered. El Salvador has the strongest guerrilla insurgency in Latin America, a seasoned force able to strike at major military installations. Violations of human rights continue at a high level. The United States continues to be the chief arbiter of power in the country. Duarte could not survive for a month if Washington withdrew its military, economic, and diplomatic support.

An editor of the *Columbia Journalism Review* offers a persuasive explanation for the disappearance of El Salvador from the U.S. media.[1] Reporting of foreign events in the U.S. press, he says, is governed by three basic principles. The press dislikes stalemates, and the conflict between the U.S.-backed military and the popular forces has long been stalemated and shows every indication that it will so continue. The press dislikes routine, and recently the death squads have been disappearing or killing only ordinary Salvadorans, no bishops, no U.S. nuns or newsmen. The press dislikes consensus, and aid to Duarte's government and the Salvadoran military meets no major opposition in Congress. "Washington's passion is instead reserved for Nicaragua. So is the media's."

These principles reflect the perception of the owners of the media as to what wins readers or listeners. They are unrelated to the national interest. What is happening in El Salvador is or should be of as much concern to us today as it was when that country made front-page news. The popular forces constitute by far the strongest guerrilla insurgency in Latin America. Human rights violations are still systematic and part of a military strategy, particularly of the air force. Death squads continue to operate. The judicial system is virtually nonfunctional for crimes of political violence. No military officer has been convicted for any of the 60,000 civilian deaths that human rights groups attribute to the government or government-condoned groups, nor have any air-force officers been disciplined for indiscriminate bombing, even in those cases in which the Armed Forces admitted responsibility and offered compensation. What happens in El Salvador should also concern us because of the heavy U.S. presence. The United States is the chief arbiter of power in the country, its fiscal 1988 contribution of over $600 million making El Salvador the second-largest per capita recipient of U.S. aid after Israel.

Given the extent to which the U.S. administration can determine what the citizens should know about foreign policy and the principles by which the media judge world events newsworthy, it is hardly surprising that the vast majority of U.S. voters don't know or don't really care which side we are on in Nicaragua or El Salvador. Neither do they know or care that violations of human rights are far worse in Guatemala than in any other country of Central America.

Behind the smokescreen of manipulated news, nevertheless, we do have a consistent policy, one on which the two parties that monopolize the national political space, have consistently maintained a consensus for a century and a half. The same basic assumptions about the way we should deal with Third World countries are shared by liberals and conservatives in the two major political parties. They believe that these countries will gradually overcome their backwardness if only they allow themselves to be incorporated more fully into our economic system and way of life, a process we in our generosity are ready to accelerate by modest injections of economic aid to be allocated in ways we alone are competent to decide.

Liberals and conservatives are likewise agreed that revolutionary movements are bad, that they spring not from internal causes but from interference by what President Reagan calls "the evil empire," and that revolution will inevitably end up as communism. No attempt is made to determine what communism is, or if such a system exists. At best, it is assumed that it is the system established in Russia by the Bolsheviks in 1917, a system endowed with mystic powers so that one communist can infect a whole barrel of democrats. Nor does anyone remember that the policy being defended predates the arrival of the Bolsheviks. In the nineteenth century, the enemy in Central America was England. After 1900 it became Germany. The Soviet menace came into being only after World War I.

Another and still stranger element in the national consensus on foreign policy is that the way to combat this ideology and prevent radical social change is not by rational discussion and the submission of the alternatives to the test of experience, but by the use of military force. That is to say, the

United States can use military force when it so decides. It can intervene in El Salvador or Nicaragua at will, but no other nation has the same right.

The steps by which this policy has been refined since its first formulation by President James Monroe in 1823 and the historic incidents that determined its growth have recently been reviewed by Professor Walter LaFeber of Cornell University.[2] The Roosevelt Corollary, formulated by President Theodore Roosevelt in 1905, two years after he had engineered the secession of Panama from Colombia, proclaimed that henceforth the United States would act as the policeman to maintain order in the hemisphere. Roosevelt played a major role in creating the U.S. image of Latin Americans who sought social change. They were "small bandit nests of a wicked and inefficient type," too lazy to get ahead by doing an honest day's work and obviously enemies of the United States. The Roosevelt Corollary was a complete reversal of the original Monroe Doctrine. It had sought to protect Latin Americans from outside—European—influence so that they could make their own decisions. The revised form declared that Latin Americans must be controlled by outside—United States—decisions.

The resulting situation was described by Under-Secretary of State Robert Olds in 1927: "We do control the destinies of Central America, and we do so for the simple reason that the national interest absolutely dictates such a course.... Until now, Central America has always understood that governments which we recognize and support stay in power, while those we do not recognize and support fail."

The rationale for this policy was well expressed in March 1938 by Bernard Baruch, who was then spokesman for Wall Street, in a memorandum to Secretary of State Cordell Hull in which he warned of the threat to the United States created by Mexico's expropriation of U.S.-owned oil properties. "The money involved is important, but it is not important compared with something of deeper significance. The ownership, control, and direction of the natural resources such as those are important to America (i.e., the United States) because they bring not only these raw materials, but the profits therefrom, increasing the American (i.e., U.S.) standards of living.... If this condition spreads to Central and South American countries, America (United States) may readily find herself not only denuded of the investment represented but also shut off from the supply of those materials, except at prices that can be dictated by others."[3]

Assistant Secretary of State for Latin America Edward Miller in May 1950 presented a new formulation which became known as the Miller Doctrine. It anticipated by 18 years its Russian counterpart, the Brezhnev Doctrine which justified collective "socialist" intervention to protect the Soviet bloc from Western influences. Starting from the position that the American hemisphere was threatened by communism, Miller asserted that the American nations were authorized by the Rio Pact of 1947 and the Charter of the Organization of American States (OAS) to intervene in any country unable to defend itself. The United States, he believed, could always control a majority of the OAS members and consequently could use the OAS to protect its interests. However, he added, if that didn't work, the United States still reserved the right to intervene unilaterally.[4]

The theory of the nation state, which in principle underlies the relations between sovereign states, presumes an absolute equality of all states. Power is, nevertheless, a reality that cannot be ignored. Stronger states have always used pressures, diplomatic, economic, even military, to impose their will on weaker neighbors. Some may think Jeane Kirkpatrick a little hysterical when she asserts that Central America is the most important place in the world for the United States today, but given the world in which we live, I think most would agree that the United States has legitimate interests to protect there, interests that can even be protected militarily to the extent that our treaty obligations with the OAS and the United Nations permit.

What we have done and continue to do, however, goes far beyond any justifiable protection of our interests. We have consistently opposed every expression of the popular will in the region, every attempt to correct utterly inequitable socioeconomic structures. The Guatemala experience is here illustrative. In 1944 for the first time, spurred by the ideals of the Atlantic Charter, Guatemala held free elections, a process it repeated until the United States ended it after a single decade.

Presidential memoirs are seldom a source of history, but the account President Dwight D. Eisenhower gives of this incident in his Memoirs is worth reading. The challenge to Guatemalan democracy came when President Jacobo Arbenz, in implementing a land reform law, expropriated—with compensation—idle lands owned by the United Fruit Company. A mercenary force put together by the Guatemalan oligarchy with United Fruit and CIA collaboration was about to collapse after Arbenz's airforce shot down the planes it had sent to bomb the capital. At this juncture, Eisenhower met with two advisers, Secretary of State John Foster Dulles, and brother Alan Dulles, head of the CIA. Both had major United Fruit interests and associations. In a couple of hours, without consulting with the President's Latin American experts, the National Security Council, or congressional leaders, they decided to replace the destroyed planes.

It was a momentous decision, one not communicated to the U.S. public even after it was implemented. It continues today to weigh heavily on the people of Guatemala and on the people of the United States. The military dictatorships that replaced the nascent democracy have slaughtered more than a hundred thousand men, women, and children, many burned alive, others barbarously tortured. In implementing ethnocidal processes, they have displaced a million and a half Indians from their homes, starving unknown numbers to death in consequence. They have trained an army to treat every civilian as an enemy and taught its shock troops to see themselves as "machines to kill."

How can one measure what that means in terms of the destruction of the social fabric of Guatemala? For the first time, a movement was developing within a segment of the oligarchy that saw the need for a more equitable distribution of the national income in the interests of social harmony. It was a period of prosperity when change could be effected with minimum sacrifice. It would be fair to say that Arbenz and his advisers were reading the signs of the times, seeking to stem a tide of revolution by hearing the cries of the people for land and a roof over their heads. Washington would recognize the principle a few years later, after Castro had consolidated his revolution in Cuba, and propose in the Alliance for Progress a vast hemispheric project of coprosperity. But for Guatemala it was too late. The forces of reaction were in control. And while Washington might express verbal disapproval of their excesses, it would no more use its political, economic, and diplomatic—not to say its military—power against them than it is willing today to use that power against tyranny in South Africa.

As in Guatemala, so in its neighbors, the determining factor in U.S. policy has similarly always been to ensure regimes amenable to our interests as defined by the decision-making groups in the United States. As control of these groups has passed progressively to the banking and financial community, the controllers of credit, the primary concern of U.S. policy has been to maintain an absolute freedom for the use and movement of capital. This concern has translated itself into a new version of capitalism, the so-called neoliberalism. It differs from classical capitalism, which recognized the existence of the poor even if it deplored the necessity of feeding them, by ignoring their existence.

Pinochet's Chile was the first state to formalize this concept. In December 1973, five months after the counterrevolution in which Salvador Allende died, I wrote that Milton Friedman's "Chicago Boys" were introducing an economy for six million people in a country that then had ten million and was experiencing population growth. I recently mentioned this comment to a Chilean social scientist who since that time has lived in exile in Central America. "Today," he said, "it has become an economy for three million in a country of twelve million. Yes, this is new, the exclusion of the poor. And we have exactly the same policy here in Central America. It is ironic. Economists of the neoliberal school condemn any state planning. Yet they themselves, at their computers, decide who shall live, who die."

In 1979, this time stirred by the ousting from Nicaragua of long-time client Somoza, Washington expressed an interest in supporting controlled social change in El Salvador to head off the threat of "another Nicaragua." But it was too late to domesticate the popular movements which, with the approval of Archbishop Romero, had taken to the streets in massive peaceful protests. They wanted too much. They wanted the fair elections they had never known. Washington, however, was not interested in fair elections. It knew they would bring to power a coalition committed to revolutionary social changes that would not favor the perceived interests of the United States.

By early 1980, the streets of San Salvador were running with the blood of unarmed civilians shot down by the armed forces at the service of the oligarchy. In each month of that year, the army and right-wing death squads operating in collaboration with it killed an average of a thousand Salvadoran men, women, and children. These killings were not in response to guerrilla actions. It was not until August that the guerrillas initiated military operations in an effort to protect the peaceful protesters.

Archbishop Romero's turn came while he was saying Mass on 24 March. The previous month he had urged the U.S. president to stop sending arms that were being and would be used to kill his people. On 23 March he had told the soldiers that God's commandment, "Thou shalt not kill," is higher than any human law. In a grotesque parody of a pagan ritual, the army killed more than twenty of the mourners at Romero's funeral Mass.

The election of Ronald Reagan as U.S. president in November 1980 gave the green light for an escalation of barbarity. Troops surrounded a Jesuit high school in San Salvador, 28 November, allowing death squad operatives to enter and drag out six top opposition politicians who were openly meeting there. Their tortured and mutilated bodies lay in the street the next day. Three days later it was the turn of four U.S. women, three of them religious, the other a lay missionary, at least two of them raped before being killed. This did indeed bring a reaction from one of the president-elect's top advisers. "We have to understand," said Jeane Kirkpatrick, who would shortly be named Ambassador to the United Nations, "that these women were not just religious; they were political activists." She was defining the parameters the new administration would allow the Salvadoran oligarchy. Any "political activist" could be shot without trial, no questions asked. In fact, not a single Salvadoran officer or death squad member has been punished for these or the other thousands of civilian killings since 1980.

The Salvadoran army is prepared to continue this war for as long as it takes to break the popular will. Such is the message Colonel Mauricio Vargas, its chief ideologue, gave me in April 1987, while he was in the field directing yet another "major offensive" in Northern Morazán. It was also the message Ambassador Corr asked me to take back to the United States. Before we met, I had learned that when he became ambassador to El Salvador two years earlier, he was projecting that the war would be won in two years. In April 1987, his projection was for another eight years.

Yet even that projection was conditional. "The guerrillas say they have a long popular warfare," he told me. "President Duarte says that he has a long strategy for peace. And I say that the American (i.e., U.S.) people should get a prolonged strategy to promote and consolidate democracy in Central America. If we're going to do it every fiscal year, every time we turn around, you know, we just complicate the problems here."[5]

Under the Reagan administration, ambassadors in Central America lose their jobs for a single public deviation from official policy. It is legitimate to assume, then, that Ambassador Corr was telling me what he was told to tell journalists. It was a straightforward message. Let Congress give the administration a blank check for as long as it takes, no more explanations to be demanded at budget time for free-fire zones, scorched-earth campaigns, destruction of crops and animals, bombing or strafing of civilians. The armed forces, as the Doctrine of National Security teaches, are the best judges of means and ends. If the U.S. public just stops interfering through its elected representatives, they will consolidate democracy in Central America.

A few days after my meeting with Ambassador Corr, a top leader of the FDR, the political counterpart of the popular armed forces, not only confirmed that the FDR does have a long-term strategy, but that its timetable is the same as the ambassador's. In his opinion, it would take the United States eight years to recognize that a military victory was impossible and finally agree to the demand of the Salvadoran people to find a political solution.

More recently the congressional hearings on the diversion of funds from secret deals with Iran to the contras, in an effort to get round congressional prohibitions, has shed new light on the extent to which Washington policy makers are prepared to go behind the backs of the U.S. public. But this is nothing new, as earlier dealings with Nicaragua demonstrate. Washington steadily backed Somoza in the late 1970s, even after all U.S. allies had repudiated him. When in 1979 it was clear that his empire was collapsing, it struggled desperately to substitute another member of the oligarchy who would continue to use Somoza's hated National Guard to protect its perceived interests. It was too late. A massive popular uprising carried the Sandinistas at the head of a broad coalition to a military victory.

The Sandinistas were not militarily naive. They had learned from Chile that the social changes they had promised the people could not be implemented as long as the oligarchy had its own army. They disbanded the National Guard, imprisoning those who had not escaped to Honduras. They had learned from Cuba that the United States would use every available means to prevent the creation of a socialist state in the region. They desperately wanted and needed good relations with the United States. The entire infrastructure, autos, buses, machines, all was U.S.-made and needed U.S. maintenance, spares, and replacements. At the same time, the Sandinistas had made a commitment they were determined to keep. The national resources would be utilized to provide an acceptable quality of life for all Nicaraguans.

Jesuit Xabier Gorostiaga, Latin America's premier economist, formulated a program that the government hoped would permit social reform with minimal challenge to Washington's perceived interests. Gorostiaga was Minister of Planning in 1979 and 1980, and he continues to act as the government's chief adviser on economic issues. His plan called for a mixed economy. Sixty percent would remain in private hands, regulated only to the extent necessary to satisfy the basic needs of all before providing luxuries for some. Half of the 40 percent inherited from Somoza and those who fled with him would remain in state ownership. This is a considerably smaller percentage of state ownership of the nation's resources than in the United States. The other half would be converted into cooperatives.

As Gorostiaga's plan was gradually implemented between 1979 and 1983, it produced a striking growth in the gross national product and in its equitable redistribution. Since then, however, U.S. hostility, expressed in economic and political measures and in the arming, training, and supplying of a mercenary force engaged in sabotage and in terrorist attacks on civilians, has paralyzed the project. It continues, nevertheless, as official policy. The most important modification has been an increase in the cooperative sector at the expense of the state sector. This is consonant with the findings of another priest, sociologist François Houtart, a professor at the University of Louvain, Belgium, who has for several years been studying land reform in Nicaragua. "To my surprise," he told me, "our studies revealed that cooperative workers quickly identified with the objectives of the revolution, with significant increase in their commitment and output; whereas state employees retained the adversarial relations with the new boss they had with the old, an attitude that negatively affected their productivity. This is an important challenge to Soviet theory and practice, with their emphasis on state ownership."[6]

Washington, nevertheless, insists that this effort by a tiny nation, lacking any offensive capability, to become master of its own destiny, is an aggression against the United States and a threat to our national security. In this stand, it has isolated itself from and lost the moral support of most of Latin America and its major European allies. It has gone against formal rulings of both the Organization of American States and of the United Nations. It has ignored the ruling of the World Court and rejected its jurisdiction, branding itself as a violator of international law. And the congressional investigations during 1987 of the Iran-Contragate scandal exposed the continuing readiness of the administration to flout Congress and involve itself with international terrorism.

Two questions immediately suggest themselves. What is the logic of the U.S. administration's attitudes and actions? and what motivates the people of Guatemala, El Salvador, and Nicaragua to continue their struggle against an aggressor so ruthless and powerful? The latter question I shall try to answer in the next chapter in a review of the changed role of the church which has moved from the margin to the center in the life-and-death struggle that engulfs Central America. The other question will be the subject of a later chapter.

Notes

1. Michael Massing, *Columbia Journalism Review*, May/June 1987, p. 21.

2. *Inevitable Revolutions*. New York: Norton, 1983.

3. Quoted in David Green, *The Containment of Latin America*. Chicago: Quadrangle Books, 1971, p. 33.

4. Department of State Bulletin # 23 (15 May 1950), 768-770.

5. This is the one statement he authorized me to quote and attribute when I interviewed him in the Embassy in San Salvador, April 1987.

6. Interview at Louvain-la-Neuve, Belgium, October 1986.

4.

The Church Changes Sides

In December 1945 I went to Havana, Cuba, to the first Catholic Inter-American Social Action Congress. Two famous U.S. priests, Jesuit John LaFarge, then editor of *America* magazine, and Raymond McGowan, head of the Social Action Department of the National Catholic Welfare Conference, had convened it. It assembled two delegates from every country and territory in the Americas. I then lived in Trinidad and attended as a representative of the Archbishop of Port of Spain.

The week-long meeting revealed some important facts about the Catholic church in Latin America. Social concerns were so low on the agenda of bishops that not a single one bothered to attend. For almost all the participants, the church was facing only two serious challenges, both intramural: a shortage of priests, and the growing Protestant penetration of a region in which it had always asserted its religious monopoly. Nobody expressed concern about the need for land reform, the rapid population growth without a corresponding expansion of the economy, or the social issues raised by urbanization.

All of this was consonant with the history of the church in Latin America. It had arrived as a department of the Spanish (and Portuguese) monarchy, charged with the specific tasks of caring for the health and education of the relatively small part of the population needed as a service sector for the oligarchy. Beyond that, its role was limited to socializing the masses into acceptance of their obligation to serve, using the sacraments and other sacred symbols to sanction its authority and that of the state. In return, it received generous financial support, and the bishops and higher clergy became honorary members of the oligarchy.

Exceptions occurred all through the colonial period. Bartolomé de las Casas, a Dominican priest, carved for himself a place in history by his long struggle to persuade the Spanish crown to put an end to the violence, harm, and suffering "more acute than ever before seen or heard," which the Spaniards had inflicted on the Indians, "the rightful owners of these kingdoms and lands." And for a century and a half the Jesuits created in a large part of what is now Paraguay, Argentina, and Brazil a society in which the Indians were the beneficiaries of their own work and developed a highly sophisticated way of life. But these and other attempts to recognize the rights of the original inhabitants of the Americas were all thwarted by the cupidity of the invaders.

The Indians were overcome but never defeated, according to historian Enrique Dussel. "The original inhabitants of these lands resisted. The category of 'resistance' indicates a way of being in existence, of subsisting in the mimetic silence of the one who was defeated but waits his turn. We know, however, that there was never a year either during the colonial period or in the nineteenth and twentieth centuries in which some group or people of the original inhabitants did not rebel. The so-called 'indigenous rebellions' constitute a phenomenon which is being studied recently but which is not yet known as fully as it deserves. There we would find that overcome but never defeated, decimated but surviving, in every corner of our continent, in Argentina or Chile, in Brazil or the Caribbean, not to mention the region of the Andes and that of Central America and Mexico, they survive, and that must not be overlooked.

"The 'resistance' of almost five centuries was, in consequence, always dialectically linked to the 'emergency.' They 'emerge' in rebellions, in their obstinate determination to remain different. Today in Guatemala, as in the times of Tumac Amaru, they rebel again, and again are massacred by the whites and mestizos, children who have forgotten their mother."[1]

Separation from Spain in the nineteenth century caused some temporary breaches in the church-state alliance. Rome, more anxious to maintain good relations with a powerful Spain than with the distant ex-colonies, long refused to accord the new governments the privileges it had granted the Spanish crown. Many of the clergy, especially at the higher levels, were Spanish and most of them returned to Spain. In addition, no bishops were named for many years, until finally Rome agreed to authorize the new governments to name the bishops, as Spain had done. The result was a serious weakening of the power of the church. Even after this problem was solved, anticlerical governments took action to reduce the wealth and influence of the church still further. Nicaragua, for instance, late in the nineteenth century confiscated all church properties, expelled all religious orders and congregations, and twice exiled the country's only bishop. Not until the U.S.-supported coup d'état of 1909, which brought a conservative regime to power, was a new equilibrium established, the church regaining its substantive privileges and in return once more legitimating the regime. Gradually in each country similar accommodations produced similar results.

The church-state clash in Nicaragua since the Sandinista revolution triumphed in 1979 has interesting parallels with this earlier conflict. While the new government treated the church much more respectfully than on the former occasion, it insisted that the church no longer be a state within the state, enjoying special privileges not given to other churches or groups. The church leaders reacted by refusing to legitimate the government and by claiming in practice not to be bound by its laws. Thus, the bishops denounced compulsory military service as a violation of the rights of the conscripts, at a time when the right of states to draft youths into the armed forces is universally acknowledged. The archdiocese of Managua asserted the right to publish a newspaper and to operate a radio transmitter without the registration process required by law.

Costa Rica's experience has always been somewhat different from that of its neighbors, and this also emerged at the Havana meeting. Father Benjamín Núñez told us how the church had taken the lead in challenging the Marxist unions that had established a monopoly during the recently ended World War II in which the Soviet Union had been allied with the Western powers. The Rerum Novarum unions were becoming—as they soon became—the dominant force in organized labor. The subsequent evolution, however, also shows the limits to Costa Rica's difference. A military coup in 1948 brought to power a liberal regime which introduced the advanced social legislation that has since distinguished Costa Rica. Without protest from the Vatican about a priest engaging in politics, Núñez became labor minister and later ambassador to the United Nations, and control of the Rerum Novarum trade unions passed from the church to the Liberal Party. The bishops reverted to their traditional activities and there they have since stayed, enjoying their state-paid salaries and their diplomatic immunities. Some priests well-placed in the church hierarchy, in addition to their other perks, augment their income by turning over a duty-free automobile every two years.

As in Costa Rica in 1945, so in all Latin America since World War II, various ideologies have fought for the allegiance of organized labor, with the Cold War as a focus and the church gradually changing its role to the extent that it has since withdrawn from its traditional alliance with reactionary governments. I was involved in another round of this conflict later in the 1940s when I went to Caracas, Venezuela, as a participant in a congress of the Inter-American Press Association (IAPA). We were lobbied by representatives of the World Federation of Trade Unions (WFTU) and the International Confederation of Free Trade Unions (ICFTU). The ICFTU is dominated by the U.S. AFL-CIO, its biggest member. It is the capitalist international trade union body; while the WFTU is the socialist. Most of the Latin Americans preferred the WFTU, but concerted pressure by the U.S. delegates, whose financial support was critical to the survival of the IAPA, carried the day. Since that time, the IAPA has consistently supported and defended dictatorships and other reactionary governments and movements in Latin America.

In 1962 the United States moved to strengthen its hold on organized Latin American labor. The obvious objective from the outset was to ensure that its leaders identify with U.S. political and economic interests. Gradually, however, it became evident that religion was a major factor in the struggle to control labor, as in other aspects of Latin American society. At first, the church seemed to oppose U.S. objectives, but later the church-related unions shifted to the right and often found themselves in alliance with the ICFTU. The first major U.S. intervention was to create the American Institute for Free Labor Development (AIFLD). Sponsored by AFL-CIO, it had the financial support of USAID, the State Department, W.R. Grace, ITT, EXXON, Shell, Kennecott, Anaconda, American Smelting and Refining, IBM, Koppers, Gillette and 85 other large corporations with Latin American interests. Its undeclared objective was to enable U.S. companies, in collaboration with repressive governments, to substitute company unions for independent ones. Peter Grace, its first and long-time board chairman, put it well: "It reaches workers to increase their company's business." More than nine-tenths of its declared annual $6 million budget came from the U.S. Treasury, and reports from serious U.S. sources have indicated additional financing by the CIA. The funds were used over the years to train several hundred thousand union members at the AIFLD's Front Royal School in Virginia, where they were indoctrinated with pro-U.S., anticommunist propaganda. AIFLD money was also used to support military coups in Guatemala, Brazil, and Chile, and in the terrorism and racial violence that dragged down the leftist government of Cheddi Jagan in Guyana.[2]

With the growth of Christian Democratic parties in Western Europe and their importation to Latin America in the late 1940s and 1950s, a third contender for the allegiance of labor entered the field, the International Federation of Christian Trade Unions (IFCTU). They created CLAT (Central Latinoamericana de Trabajadores) to compete with AIFLD for the allegiance of Latin America's workers. The United States at first opposed the newcomer whose main funding came from the Konrad-Adenauer-Stiftung, an agency of the German Christian Democrat party, because it took an anti-U.S. position that favored the interests of West Germany. The Socialist and the Christian Internationals and their affiliates were agreed in those days on the basic postulate that the function of the trade union in Latin America was largely—if not primarily—political; that social structures had to be changed before unions could acquire bargaining power. The AIFLD, on the contrary, claimed that trade unionism would succeed in Latin America by imitating its experience in the United States where labor had prospered by staying out of politics and concentrating on the strictly economic issues of wages, working conditions, health and pension benefits, and so forth. As the Christian Democrats moved to the right, however, both the AIFLD and big business have sought better relations with the IFCTU, recognizing that its close association with conservative elements in the church made it a potential ally in the struggle to win hearts and minds.

The late 1950s saw the beginning of a major change in the life of the church in Latin America when Pope Pius XII appealed to the United States and other missionary-sending churches to allocate ten percent of their priests and sisters to Latin America. Many who responded had been expelled from China and nearly all arrived with the traditional concepts of the missionary's role. For most from the United States, this meant creating in Latin America U.S.-style parishes to serve as pilot projects which the Latin Americans themselves would embrace and replicate.

This model quickly proved itself dysfunctional. The society lacked the economic base for such structures. A parish plant, with church, rectory, parish hall, gymnasium, and school, even if built with external funds, served only a privileged handful in a parish of a hundred thousand faithful spread over a vast area. Many missionaries gradually reached the conclusion that radical social change should be a top priority, on the ground that people must live as humans before they can live as Christians.

The updated self-image achieved by the church at the Second Vatican Council (1962-1965) strengthened such attitudes. The stress on service to humankind, and especially to the poor, encouraged the trend to give preference to social action over traditional religious activities. The emphasis on the primacy of the local church helped foreign missionaries to recognize that their attempt to impose the structures and attitudes of their home churches was a form of colonialism. Such self-questioning was greatly encouraged and offered new perspectives by an article entitled "The Vanishing Clergyman"[3] published by Ivan Illich who, as head of the Cuernavaca Institute, had introduced many U.S. missionaries to the Spanish language and Latin American culture. The Roman Catholic church, said Illich, is "the world's largest nongovernmental bureaucracy," employing 1.8 million full-time workers. For all its efficiency, people "suspect that it has lost its relevance." The traditional clergyman is a "folkloric phantom," a "member of the aristocracy of the only feudal power remaining in the world," a "man sentenced to disappear, whether the church wishes it or not, by the changes in modern society." Instead, Illich saw the leisure society as opening a part-time ministry to laymen "mature in Christian wisdom" through prayer, study of scripture, and a life of service, without removal from their careers or incorporation into a clerical caste. Illich's prophecy has not yet been implemented in the so-called leisure—or better, consumer—society, but it is a remarkable anticipation of what would soon happen in the slums and villages of Latin America with the flowering of the Christian base communities that have played a key role in the development of the popular movements in many parts of Central America and elsewhere.

One who has described the process of his radicalization is Thomas Melville, a Maryknoll missionary expelled from Guatemala with three colleagues—one of them his brother—after working for fifteen years among the highland Indians. They were charged with having helped a guerrilla group. "Having come to the conclusion that the actual state of violence, composed of the malnutrition, ignorance, sickness, and hunger of the vast majority of the Guatemalan population, is the direct result of a capitalist system that makes the defenseless Indian compete against the powerful and well-armed landowner, my brother and I decided not to be silent accomplices of the mass murder that this system generates. We began teaching the Indians that no one will defend their rights, if they do not defend themselves. If the government and the oligarchy are using arms to maintain them in their position of misery, then they have the obligation to take up arms and defend their God-given rights to be men.... This is a situation which is not an accident of history but an international perversion of the natural order effected by a wealthy minority, supported by the national army, which is in turn backed by the government of the United States and blessed by the hierarchy of the Catholic church.... The fact that the United States is training the armies of the countries of Latin America to help maintain the state of exploitation is a further reason why we, as citizens of the United States, should struggle to correct this shocking situation."[4]

The many experiments in new forms of church structure had one important element in common. They stressed the need for active involvement of the entire People of God, a far cry from the traditional approach which presumed a transfer of knowledge—and of the faith—from one who possessed it to others who lacked it. They also stressed the need to give practical implementation to the conclusions reached intellectually. More and more people were picking up bits of the theory elaborated by Paulo Freire, the Brazilian educator who in 1964 was exiled by the military dictatorship and who for the subsequent nine years taught Chileans (and others in Chile and Peru) about "conscientization," the process by which one becomes aware of one's reality and decides to act to change it. Freire insisted that the process of learning must be linked to the social and political context of the learner. The conventional transfer of information from an all-knowing teacher to a passive recipient he rejected as indoctrination rather than learning.

I observed this process of conscientization and its effects in several countries of Latin America in the late 1960s. A trained pastoral worker, sometimes a priest, more often a nun, occasionally a lay leader, would assemble a small group in a slum. They would pray, read the scriptures, discuss their concerns, and work on some community problem, the water supply, a school, a bridge, whatever they agreed the community most needed. Certain sections of scripture evoke an intense response from people who have never before been exposed to them. Exodus, the story of the political and religious liberation of a mass of slaves, who through the power of a covenant with God, become God's chosen people, is particularly challenging. In the Prophets they identify an uncompromising defence of God as liberator, a vigorous denunciation of injustice, an open assertion of the rights of the poor, and the assurance that those faithful to justice will be appropriately awarded. In the gospels they are confronted with a Jesus, a savior, who announces that the moment of liberation from physical and spiritual evils has arrived, who acts to implement his promises, and who gives meaning to history by his death and resurrection. Then we have The Acts of the Apostles which describe the life of an ideal Christian community that holds all things in common, and Revelation which portrays in symbolic terms the final successful struggle of the people of God against the monsters of power and deception.

Reflection on the state of oppression in which the poor exist in the light of what scripture tells them leads to a critical analysis of its causes. The conclusion expressed by the bishops of Latin America at Puebla, Mexico, in 1979, follows, namely, that poverty is conflictive, "not a passive phase (but...) the product of economic, social, and political situations and structures... where the rich get richer at the expense of the poor, who get even poorer."[5] The poor have now reached a dialectical or historico-structural explanation of their poverty as the product of the way society is organized to exploit some of its members by denying them a fair share of the wealth created by their work and to exclude others—the unemployed and the marginalized—from the production process and its benefits.

Discussion still continues as to whether such base communities are viable and appropriate for the middle classes. Up to now, at least, they are effectively confined to the very poor, the marginal in society. They are, nevertheless, by no means an expression of inevitable class warfare in the sense in which their opponents formulate the Marxist concept. Neither are they divisive, as conservative Christians claim. They constitute rather what the Scholastics called the actus primus (the first moment) of doing theology, of seeking to determine each one's role in the work of creation as intended by a loving God. It is a diffuse and generalized theology based on the logic of life as actually experienced by the poor, an experience interpreted in the light of scriptural paradigms within and with the help of a community of people of like mind and like living conditions. But these bases are always connected through bishops, priests, nuns, and other pastoral workers with the wider community of faith, a community that in turn is related to and enriched by the community of professional theologians with their critical methods, their systematic analysis, and their synthesis.[6]

Much speculation similarly exists about the objective societal conditions that encourage the growth of these base communities. In Guatemala and in Nicaragua under Somoza, as in Brazil under the military dictatorship, a major factor would seem to be the destruction of other social structures, labor unions, student organizations. In Guatemala, in particular, the killing or expulsion of many priests and nuns left the lay leaders they had trained with no alternative but to meet informally, if not secretly, with their neighbors and lead them in prayer and study of the scriptures. The fact that in Indian communities the same person traditionally presided at both community and religious events facilitated the substitution of the village leader for the absent priest and also facilitated the evolution of the base community from a purely religious role to that of a leading agent for change, at first by peaceful methods, then often under repression in armed struggle. In El Salvador, Indians had effectively disappeared as an identifiable culture, but their traditions survive and have worked in the same direction. Even in these societies, however, there seem to be few if any instances of spontaneous emergence of Christian base communities. A priest or other trained pastoral worker started the process, and soon it took on its own independent life.

This is, of course, the radical change in the church in Latin America since 1945, a change that is responsible for the emergence of the people of Central America as the new historic subject committed to take control of its own destiny. From what has been said above it is clear that the Christian base community movement and the Theology of Liberation are closely linked in something of a chicken-and-egg relationship. Gustavo Gutiérrez, who ought to know, says that the Theology of Liberation is the systematized formulation of the theological wisdom generated in the Christian base communities. It seems clear in any case that the two movements are reciprocally supportive and mutually enriching.

The evolution of the internal dynamic of these communities within a broad diversity of social contexts and conflicts has been quite consistent. Each begins with usually a fairly extensive period of prayer, bible study, and analysis, and modest tasks of community improvement and mutual support. Then, as their attempts to acquire some control over their own lives, to speak for themselves and grasp a share of power, come up against vested interests and produce a reaction of repression, they respond with growing militancy. What started as a religious commitment takes on political overtones. The base communities do not themselves become political movements nor do they ally formally with political movements. But their members incorporate themselves into whatever organizations are available that they judge will promote the objectives they seek. In this way, in Somoza's Nicaragua, the base communities provided many of the militants for the Sandinistas, and after the Triumph they provided many of the leaders at all levels of the revolutionary government. Similarly, they have long formed and continue to form the broad social base of support that enables the popular forces in El Salvador to sustain the war now in its ninth year.

Perhaps nowhere more than in the Indian towns and villages of the Guatemalan highlands is the dynamic role of the base communities observable. Here since the early 1970s the ethnocidal oppression by the army and the death squads has been accompanied by a parallel growth of base communities, the Delegate of the Word or the catechist being almost invariably the village leader responsibie for supervising all community activities, including the appropriate measures—unarmed or armed—to provide protection against the army and death squads.

One Indian, survivor of massacres and death squads, described for me with extraordinary clarity how the experience had developed a new sense of what it means to be a Christian. "It is as though our very poverty, our want, the need to keep fleeing, not to be tied down by anything, is enabling us to work more and more as a group. We no longer plant separately, we all plant and harvest as a group, and each takes as much as the family needs, not even measuring or weighing. Before, we had villages and towns. We had mayors, governors, and priests. Now we organize ourselves. The elected representatives determine the tasks of each, the various activities of production and marketing, education, care of the sick, the lookouts to warn if the army is coming."

In Central America, as in all Latin America, this movement has given the church a broad popular base it previously lacked. It has also resulted in an enormous release of emotional energy that has expressed itself in the political as well as in the religious sphere. Washington is seriously concerned. As far back as 1969, the Rockefeller Report warned that the United States could no longer count automatically, as it previously could, on the support of the church in Latin America. Soon after, in 1975, the CIA produced the Banzer Plan, first floated in Bolivia by the Interior Ministry of right-wing dictator Hugo Banzer. It sought by "dirty tricks" to smear and harass progressive church leaders. "The church as an institution should not be attacked, but only a part of the church, the vanguard. Propaganda should emphasize that certain foreign mission groups known for their commitment to social change had been sent... for the exclusive purpose of directing the church toward communism."[7] The plan called for a central depository of intelligence containing dossiers on all progressive laity, clergy, and bishops. The CIA was particularly valuable in "providing full information on certain priests—personal data, studies, friends, addresses, writings, contacts abroad, etc."

By 1980, President-elect Reagan's advisers were insisting that the United States must actively combat the theology of liberation as a threat to U.S. interests. Since that time, the fundamentalist ultraright has been flooding Latin America, especially Central America, with preachers endowed with the vast financial resources generated by the electronic churches in the United States. Their "revivalist" techniques quickly won them many adherents among peasants who were nominally Catholic but who in practice had little association with the church as an institution. In Nicaragua, which was a special target of these fundamentalists, the number of Protestants rose from 74,400 in 1979 to 376,900 in 1982. The growth has since continued, raising the Protestant population from 3 percent in 1979 to 15 percent by 1985. Whatever their intentions, their message of an otherworldly gospel and of obedience to rulers, a rehash of what the Catholic church in Latin America had traditionally taught, is objectively a powerful support of the oligarchy in those countries in which the oligarchy still controls and of the U.S. defense of the status quo. In Nicaragua they discourage their members from participating in the social programs promoted by the government, including the literacy and health campaigns and the volunteer harvest brigades. Many of them also resist the compulsory military service instituted in 1983.

The emergence of the Christian base communities in the late 1960s was greeted approvingly by most Latin American bishops. After all, the inspiration and guidance had come from the official pastoral workers, the loyalty of whom had not then been questioned. The historic meeting of the bishops at Medellín, Colombia, in 1968, which called for "global, daring, urgent, and basically renewing change," spoke approvingly of them. The subsequent bishops' meeting at Puebla, Mexico, in 1979, with its stress on the church's "preferential option for the poor," again praised the base communities.

Puebla, however, added a new note. The evolution of the base communities during the 1970s had made clear that this was not just a new form of Catholic Action ready to provide foot soldiers to carry out orders and implement policies formulated by the bishops. It was, as the theologians of liberation were describing it, a new way of being church, a church born of the people. It had its own goals, revolutionary goals in the sense that they envisaged the role of the church as including the transformation of society. The bishops at Puebla, recognizing this, were at pains to insist that their authority not be challenged, that the base communities not become a parallel church.

The issue remains unresolved, and this for two reasons. First, we are dealing with two ecclesiologies, two different understandings of the nature and function of the church. The bishops—and this is particularly true of Central America, as contrasted with Brazil—see the church as a pyramid, with all the decisions made at the top by the pope and filtered through them to the lower clergy and finally to the laity. This was the theology they learned in the seminary, to the extent that they learned any theology. It was unquestioned, at least in public, from the sixteenth century Council of Trent to the Second Vatican Council in the 1960s. The base communities, their theology coming through the theology of liberation from the Second Vatican Council, see the church as a series of concentric circles, the laity as well as the clergy having active roles. They believe, as the Second Vatican Council said explicitly, that the pope and bishops do not always have the answer for each existential situation, so that it is up to the people to make their own decisions and act accordingly.

The second reason is that in Central America the bishops and the base communities represent different classes, the oligarchy and the poor. Individuals can and do transcend their class allegiances, as Archbishop Oscar Romero did in El Salvador. But sociologically speaking, each person's judgment on the reality he or she lives is conditioned by class. For one, change is threatening; for the other, survival requires change. An idealistic reading of the Gospel message has made it difficult for Christians, especially Roman Catholics, to face up to this fact. But class conflict is a fact. It was not invented by Karl Marx. "Every city," wrote Plato, "is two cities, the city of the rich and the city of the poor; and the conflict between these two never ceases." Class conflict is as old as history, and class plays a role in every judgment.

The conflict in Central America is obviously complicated by the existence of these two divergent ways of being church. In San Salvador, in November 1985, I participated for a long day in a meeting of one hundred leaders of base communities, representing the principal conglomerations of slums in and around the city. Archbishop Rivera Damas came for two hours in midmorning. His 20-minute talk and questions and statements from the floor which occupied the rest of the time focused on a single issue: the danger (as the bishop saw it), and the need (as the people saw it) of supporting the popular forces in their struggle against the oligarchy and the U.S.-supported armed forces. The archbishop insisted that his role as impartial negotiator would be jeopardized by the alliance. The base community leaders saw support of the popular forces as their overriding obligation. The exchange ended in a draw. Small group discussions in which I participated later in the day made it clear that nobody had been converted.

The stand-off continues today, as recent conversations with representatives of both sides indicate. One priest summed up the situation well. The institutional church, he said, is like a Hovercraft. It carries on with its established activities, but it has no organic relationship with the sea two feet below, the base communities. They have their own structures and their own agenda.

Does that mean that the base communities have ceased to be church, having transformed themselves into political entities, as the Institute on

Religion and Democracy and other critics claim? I do not think so. Sociologists in the tradition of Max Weber identify the base communities as a prophetic church. They enable their members to recognize social relations, to make them meaningful as an experience of oppression and exploitation, and to learn how to overcome these conditions by human effort understood as revolutionary work. The result is an integrated worldview combined with an emotional response that has extraordinary mobilizing power. This worldview retains its religious character because it is articulated around biblical concepts that relate it to a transcendent universe.

In Nicaragua, the conflict within the church is far more acute than it is in El Salvador, and it is further complicated by the conflict between the institutional church and the revolutionary government. As in all Central American countries, the capital city in Nicaragua dominates the entire society. The institutions of the church as well as those of the government are concentrated there. In consequence, the bishop in the capital outweighs in influence all the other bishops combined. It was this fact that enabled Archbishop Romero in San Salvador to present himself publicly as the symbolic leader of reform movements, at a time when all the other Salvadoran bishops identified with the oligarchy. As archbishop of Managua, Obando y Bravo had a similar position of preeminence in the Nicaraguan church, a position further enhanced when Rome named him a cardinal. He dictates the policy of the Nicaraguan bishops vis-à-vis the revolutionary government, although at most two of the other seven bishops are fully in accord with him.

Obando was always close personally and ideologically to the anti-Somoza faction of the oligarchy, especially those members who saw the need for controlled social change in order to head off revolution. In the late 1960s, the Catholic bishops and also prominent Protestant leaders expressed strong disapproval of the repressive activities of the Somozas. In June 1979 the bishops declared that conditions for a legitimate armed insurrection existed. Obando, however, continued to hope that his reformist friends, rather than the Sandinistas who were committed to radical social change, would replace Somoza. Just a few days before Somoza fled, he was in Caracas, at the U.S. embassy, with some of these Nicaraguan friends and leaders of Venezuela's Christian Democrats, trying to negotiate such a transfer of power.

When this project failed, he seemed for a time to accept the legitimacy of the new regime, and in November 1979 he joined with the other bishops in a pastoral letter that recognized the role of the Sandinistas in leading the revolutionary process, discussed the compatibility of socialism and Christianity, and declared the new situation in Nicaragua a privileged opportunity for the church to implement the preferential option it had made for the poor.

"We are confident," the bishops wrote, "that our revolutionary process will be something original, creative, truly Nicaraguan, and in no sense imitative. For what we, together with most Nicaraguans, seek is a process that will result in a society completely and truly Nicaraguan, one that is not capitalist, nor dependent, nor totalitarian." Responding to this letter, the Sandinistas acknowledged the positive role of religious faith and institutions in motivating people to fight for justice, and they affirmed their commitment to freedom of religion.

When his two oligarchic friends resigned from the Junta in 1980, however, Obando changed his position to one of open hostility. At his prompting, the bishops criticized the Sandinista leadership for its handling of the crisis among the Miskito communities of the Atlantic coast. They also charged that the education programs of the government are in reality political indoctrination and have expressed fears about atheism and totalitarian rule. In September 1983 they denounced the newly promulgated conscription law as an attempt to mold the conscripts to Sandinista ideology, using language that was widely interpreted as a repudiation of the legitimacy of the regime. Their Easter pastoral letter of 1984 called for unconditional negotiations with the contras. Its tone was so harsh that it brought public rebuttals from the Jesuit, Dominican, and Franciscan orders in Nicaragua.

Obando showed his partiality still more openly in April 1985. On his way home from Rome where he had received the cardinal's red hat, he stopped in Miami and celebrated mass before a congregation composed largely of Nicaraguan exiles. Contra leaders Edén Pastora, Adolfo Calero, and Cristóbal Mendoza Rocha (a former Somoza security agent) were seated prominently near the altar. Not long afterward, in reply to a query about his motivation for this action, he said that he did not object to "being identified with the people who had taken up arms."

Not less significant has been Obando's refusal to protest a single one of the many fully documented atrocities committed by the contras. He has assumed the role of leader of all who share his rejection of the legitimacy of the regime. This was clear at his mass on Holy Thursday of 1987 attended by several thousand people. It was held in a gymnasium and the atmosphere was that of a political rally, loudspeakers blaring as a priest led the crowd in such slogans as *Viva Nicaragua Católica,* all code expressions to spread the message that the cardinal is defending the faith against a godless enemy. "This is like warming up for a soccer game in London," whispered an English woman who was standing beside me. "Did you ever see such a shameless prostitution of religious symbols?" asked a U.S. nun with many years of missionary work with Nicaragua's poor, as I left the gymnasium. I never have.

Obando has forced Catholics to take sides for or against the government. Publicly, all the bishops support Obando. Only one, however, Bishop Pablo Antonio Vega of Juigalpa, has shown the same extreme opposition to the Sandinistas and support for the contras. Vega was expelled from Nicaragua in July 1986 for cooperating in the United States in the Reagan administration's efforts to secure congressional funding for the contras, and for openly seditious behavior inside Nicaragua.

In March 1986 Vega had participated in a seminar in the United States with three top contra leaders, Adolfo Calero, Arturo Cruz, and Enrique Bermúdez (ex-Colonel of Somoza's National Guard). Appealing for aid for the contras, he denounced the "Sandinista persecution of religion," and asserted that the Sandinistas had killed three priests, a charge that was totally groundless. "Previously," he said, "Nicaragua's problem was underdevelopment; now, it is how to escape the Soviet bloc." Again in Washington in June 1986, he appealed for aid to the contras by saying: "In Nicaragua we have a totalitarian Marxist-Leninist regime.... Armed struggle is a human right. What other remedy remains for a people repressed not only politically but militarily?" Shortly after, at a press conference in Managua, 2 July 1986, Vega not only refused to condemn U.S. support for the contras but endorsed the "right" of the Nicaraguan people to "defend" themselves against their government. He also rejected the decision of the World Court which a week earlier had ruled that the United States was in violation of international law by "training, equipping, financing, and supplying the contras forces or otherwise encouraging, supporting, and aiding military and paramilitary activities in and against Nicaragua."[8] The decree of expulsion was issued later on the same day (2 July), immediately after the U.S. Congress had voted $103 million in aid to the contras.

Several other bishops, by contrast, have condemned the U.S. intervention. Bishop Carlos Santi of Matagalpa, discussing President Reagan's policies in December 1984, said: "I am really not in agreement with any government which intervenes in the affairs of another government.[9] "Just two days later, Bishop Pablo Schmidt of Bluefields said: "In my view, any direct aggression would be a disaster for the Nicaraguan people. As a priest, as a Capuchin, as a Christian, I cannot be in favor of U.S. intervention."[10] And a year earlier, Bishop Rubén López Ardón of Estelí had said: "All peoples have the right to free self-determination. As a sovereign and independent country, Nicaragua has this right, and everyone must respect the Nicaraguan people's right to self-determination."[11]

The conflict has divided the priests and sisters, as well as the laity. As for the laity, the division has been strictly on class lines, with the poor who constitute the vast majority solidly in support of the revolution. The priests and sisters who work directly with the poor almost all equally identify with the revolution. They constitute most of the sisters, most of the religious priests, and a minority of the diocesan priests whose training and institutional ties were with the bishops. As in much of Latin America, these diocesan priests have traditionally limited their ministry to saying mass and administering the sacraments, a ministry that was utilized by only a small minority, mostly the well-to-do. The poor majority, while committed to the practices of popular religiosity, had little formal religious practice. Few of them ever married in the church or attended mass more than once or twice a year.

Obando and some of the other bishops have used various devices to silence the priests and sisters who support the government. Diocesan priests are shifted to positions in which they can have little impact. Religious orders are pressured to remove from Nicaragua members who speak out. Sister Mary Hartman, a U.S. nun who works with the Human Rights Commission and is responsible for investigating charges of violations of the rights of prisoners, has told me that Obando asked her superior to transfer her out of Nicaragua. The superior asked him to state his reasons in writing. That was several years ago, and he has not done so.

In recent years, Obando has shown growing interest in a kind of charismatic mysticism. He has expressed his belief in the reported visions of the Virgin Mary by a campesino in Caupa, which was at that time the diocese of Bishop Vega. Vega has also shown that he accepts the visions as valid, invoking Our Lady of Caupa at the inauguration as president of Daniel Ortega in January 1985. The reported messages of the Virgin strikingly follow the Fatima model, with a creole overlay. She called for the elimination of all atheistic books from Nicaragua and for a more biblical pastoral program. She asked that two sanctuaries be built, one dedicated to Our Lady of Caupa, the other to Our Lady of Victories. Those affirming the visions interpret the "victories" as the final triumph of good over evil proclaimed in the Book of Revelations, or more concretely, as the triumph in Nicaragua of Reagan's "good empire" over the "evil empire" of communism. Finally, there is a "secret message," with as yet no indication as to when or how it will be revealed.

Obando's policies have thus involved him on two fronts. Within the church, he works to delegitimate those, including priests and sisters, who support the revolution. In his dealings with the state, he wants the contras to be accepted as a legitimate expression of popular opposition to the regime. Both positions parallel those of the United States. During and after the Pope's visit to Nicaragua in 1983, the Vatican gave many indications of support on both counts, the most striking being the naming of Obando as Central American cardinal when the more obvious and less controversial choice would have been Archbishop Rivera Damas of El Salvador. John Paul II's understanding of his role as pope, as well as his Polish experience, would incline him to support Obando, regardless of the intrinsic merits of the latter's positions. He sees the survival of the church as dependent on absolute unity under its appointed rulers, a vision of church confirmed by the success of the Polish church in maintaining its power and relative independence under a hostile Marxist regime.

The Reagan administration went to great efforts to get Vatican support for its Central American policies, especially for its commitment to oust the Sandinista-led regime. In June 1982 President Reagan and his then Secretary of State Alexander Haig visited the Vatican and expressed to the Pope their concern to stop the "spread of communist tyranny" in Latin America. The following nine months, leading up to the papal visit to Central America, saw a flurry of Washington activity in Rome. U.S. Ambassador at Large Vernon Walters, a former CIA deputy director, was there in October, followed by Secretary of State George Shultz (Haig's successor) in December. In early February 1983, just before the visit started, it was Vice-President George Bush's turn to talk both to the Pope and to Vatican Secretary of State Agostino Casaroli. The content of papal speeches in each country closely followed the official U.S. policy at that time.

In Nicaragua, in particular, the impact of the papal visit was extremely negative for the regime, in spite of the fact that the government had gone to great expense and effort in preparing a welcome. The Pope refused absolutely to pray for the victims of contra attacks, even though they included young men from Managua recently killed in the fighting. He denounced the "popular church" and told the people to obey their bishops. The papal mass, attended by some 40 percent of the country's population, was interrupted by cries of "We want peace" and countercries from a small number of Obando supporters of "Long live the Pope, long live Obando." Television beamed around the world images of an angry pope demanding silence. The press, particularly in the United States, claimed that the Sandinistas had deliberately insulted the visiting pontiff.

Vatican-Nicaragua relations probably reached their lowest point when Obando was made a cardinal in May 1985. As the new cardinal stepped up his skirmishing with the government, it responded by stopping the publication of a church weekly (*Iglesia*) which had been issued without the authorization required under state of emergency regulations, closing Radio Católica for refusing to submit its news reports for censorship, forbidding the return of Monsignor Bismarck Carballo, Obando's official spokesman, from a trip to the United States, and exiling Bishop Vega.

During 1986, nevertheless, it became evident that the Vatican was not prepared to identify totally with Obando's efforts to delegitimate the government. John Paul II is believed to have been influenced by the growing solidarity of the countries of Latin America, even those ideologically most opposed to the Sandinistas, in favor of a political solution that would leave the Sandinistas in power. Also, in April 1986, he issued a new statement on the theology of liberation which backed off from many of the earlier criticisms, to the point of asserting that the theology of liberation was not only opportune but "useful and necessary." The formal protests for the exiling of Bishop Vega were unusually mild, and the Vatican studiously ignored Vega's proposal that he be named to head a bishopric in exile. The new nuncio, Paolo Giglio, arrived in Managua in the summer with a conciliatory message for the government and soon reopened the dialogue between the bishops and the government after it had been stalled for two years.

When the talks resumed, the church wanted to limit them to specific points of conflict, dialogue with the contras, permission for Vega to return, reopening of the Catholic radio station, recognition of the church's right to publish a newspaper. The government absolutely excluded dialogue with the contras from the agenda on the ground that they constitute, not an expression of Nicaraguan opinion, but a mercenary army at the service of the United States. The other issues, it argued, could be dealt with only within the framework of an over-all church-state entente. This would include a clear acknowledgment by the church of the legitimacy of the regime, a withdrawal by Obando from his role as a rallying point for disaffected elements who are unwilling to participate in the political process, and a condemnation by the bishops of the U.S. aggression, in particular of the determining role of the United States in the contra campaign of sabotage and terrorism.

A collapse of the talks was avoided by a compromise under which the two agendas are being pursued simultaneously, although as yet without significant concrete results. Still, the mere fact of dialogue is an improvement on the earlier situation. Selection of Obando by the government as negotiator under Esquipulas II (reviewed below) has further lessened tensions. The polarization within the church, nevertheless, continues, and the impact on the new generation emerging from the universities and high schools is extremely negative. Many are simply rejecting the church as irrelevant. The peasants are torn between their traditional respect for the clergy and their commitment to the revolution. But they are very pragmatic people, as the poor must be to survive. The general attitude is that of a peasant woman who went to a health clinic for birth-control advice. Asked if she had religious objections to using contraceptives, she replied: "The pope doesn't feed my children."

In its war against the Sandinistas, the Reagan administration has devoted much effort to interpret the struggle as one of religiously motivated people against godless communists seeking to persecute and destroy religious belief. Two documents prepared as guides for the contra by the CIA advised them to accentuate religious tension. They told them, for example, to express indignation over the lack of freedom of worship in Nicaragua and to claim that priests were being persecuted. This was but part of an elaborate propaganda campaign of half-truths, distortions, and outright lies, as well as the promotion of various institutes and organizations which under the guise of religion tried to sway U.S. religious opinion. Undoubtedly, all this propaganda has had some impact but it has failed to win the support of the U.S. Catholic bishops or of the major Protestant churches for Reagan's Central American policies.

Most recently, at their November 1987 meeting in Washington, the Catholic bishops reaffirmed their earlier statements. Having praised the five Central American presidents for the wisdom and courage of making "at least more probable what was deemed almost impossible brief months ago," they repeated their support of the Central American bishops "in urging the adoption of sincere dialogue and negotiation among contending parties," and in continuing "to insist that true peace can come about only when the fundamental causes of the conflicts, especially the historic denials of social justice, are sincerely faced."

On the specific issue of U.S. administration policy toward Nicaragua, the bishops wrote: "A near exclusive focus of attention on Nicaragua and a policy debate reduced to the question of U.S. support for an armed opposition reflects, in our view, a skewed and inadequate approach.... Only a political solution can finally be successful in Nicaragua as in Central America generally; there is no politically or morally acceptable military solution. Further intensification of the military conflict must be avoided and the tide turned decisively in a new direction. We have argued that direct military aid to forces seeking the overthrow of a government with which we are not at war and with which we maintain diplomatic relations is at least legally doubtful and morally wrong. U.S. mining of Nicaraguan harbors, training and supplying of irregular forces and otherwise aggressing against a sovereign nation seem clearly to violate treaty obligations under the UN and OAS charters and the Rio Treaty, and to violate as well the principles of customary international law.... We do believe the policy of support for the contras to be morally flawed, however sincere the intentions of the persons who have crafted and implemented it."[12]

Catholic voices from the other side of the world strikingly parallel the views of the U.S. bishops. In July 1986, when Bishop Vega was exiled from Nicaragua, his fellow bishops wrote to bishops' conferences around the world asking them to protest. Some Asian bishops decided to send a delegation to study the situation for them. It included Archbishop Leobard D'Souza of Nagpur, Maharashtra, India, Bishop Miguel Mansap of Ubon, Thailand, and Sister Filo Hirota, Justice and Peace Commission, Tokyo. Each produced a separate report for incorporation into a single document that was widely distributed in eastern Asia but almost totally ignored by the media in the United States. Two short extracts from Archbishop D'Souza summarize the conclusions on which they all agreed.

"Is there religious persecution in Nicaragua? Is there lack of religious freedom? From what we saw, from the people we met, the freedom with which we were able to make contacts and move around easily, is proof that there is no religious persecution or curtailment of freedom for the church....

The government for reasons of state cannot tolerate the undermining of the sovereignty and integrity of the country. The church, however, sees an insidious move of the FSLN government to bring Nicaragua into the communist fold. From what we saw and heard there is no substance to this accusation or fear. The commitment of the FSLN to pluralism is not a façade but a reality. This is seen in the recognition of political opposition parties, the proliferation of Protestant sects, and the presence of numerous nongovernmental organizations which are working without let or hindrance."[13]

In their recent statement the U.S. bishops deplored the fact that U.S. policy downplayed or ignored the poverty, injustice, violence, excessive militarism, and rampant corruption that are widespread in Central America. One seldom hears, for example, of the violations of human rights, including religious rights, by the armed forces of Guatemala and death squads working in close collaboration with them. In that country by the 1970s the church had become a force for change through conscientization of the Indian and Ladino peasants, and it paid dearly in the reign of terror of the late 1970s and the 1980s. More than a dozen priests and hundreds of lay leaders have been killed and many more forced into exile.

Although almost totally ignored by the U.S. media and passed over in absolute silence by the U.S. administration, the reign of terror against the peasants, and in particular against the catechists and other church workers, continues unabated. A Guatemalan Justice and Peace report of July 1987 noted "continuous and systematic violation of rights and fundamental liberties of the Guatemalan people," as in previous months. The government, it said, does not work for solution of the socioeconomic structural causes but implements repressive measures that further worsen the situation of the poorest sectors of society and continues to promote civil defense patrols, development poles, and clandestine prisons. It reported seven disappearances during the previous month and sixteen assassinations by death squads. One of those assassinated was Benedicto Ortega Ordóñez, aged 22, a leader of 300 peasant families who are pursuing legal means to acquire land in Nueva Concepción, Escuintla.

The signing of Esquipulas II brought no respite. The Guatemalan Church in Exile reported in October 1987 heavy fighting in El Quiché, Ixcán region, with intensive air bombardments. The war, it said, had intensified since the Arias agreements had been signed. Also in October, Rigoberta Menchú, a Delegate of the Word whose father was burned to death in the Spanish Embassy in Guatemala City in 1980, reported in a Mexican newspaper that "the daily repression of the army against our communities continues, with bombings, toxic defoliants, forced labor, military occupation of our villages and other aggressive acts.... For fruitful dialogue, they must stop the repression, end the militarization of the country which involves civil patrols, model villages, development poles, forced military recruitment, and military control of the population."

The Guatemalan bishops try to maintain distance both from the government and from the guerrilla forces which operate in various parts of the country, while continuing to work among the Indian and Ladino poor.

One thing is clear. In the struggle to determine the future of Central America, religion occupies center stage. The contending forces are more concerned to control and manipulate the religious symbols than to occupy territory. God is still very much alive.

Notes

1. *Iglesias,* Mexico City, October 1987, p. 15.

2. *Latin American Documentation.* Washington, D.C.: U.S. Catholic Conference, Nov. 1979, pp. 1-3.

3. *The Critic.* Chicago: Thomas More Association, 1967. Reprinted in Ivan D. Illich, *Celebration of Awareness.* New York: Doubleday, 1970.

4. *National Catholic Reporter,* Kansas City, Missouri, 31 January 1968.

5. Third Conference of Latin American Bishops, Puebla, Mexico, 1979. Final Document, #1160.

6. See Leonardo and Clodovis Boff, *Introducing Liberation Theology.* Maryknoll, N.Y.: Orbis Books, 1986.

7. "The Bolivian Government Against the Church," *Latin American Documentation*. Washington, D.C.: U.S. Catholic Conference, June 1975, pp. 1-4.

8. Typed transcript of press conference provided by Centro Antonio Valdivieso, Managua.

9. *Barricada*, Managua, 18 December 1984.

10. *Barricada*, 20 December 1984.

11. *Nuevo Diario*, Managua, 6 November 1985.

12. *Origins*. Washington, D.C.: U.S. Catholic Conference, 3 December 1987. Vol. 17, # 25, pp. 441 ff.

13. Photocopy of Report in author's possession.

5.

Two Models: Life and Death

In the deafening din of conflicting interpretations of what is happening in Central America, the universal agreement on one fundamental issue can easily be overlooked. Henry Kissinger stated it clearly in the Report of the National Bipartisan Commission on Central America submitted to President Reagan in January 1984.

The violent upheavals in Central America, the Report says, are rooted in poverty and repression. "Discontents are real, and for much of the population conditions of life are miserable; just as Nicaragua was ripe for revolution, so the conditions that invite revolution are present elsewhere in the region as well."[1]

The Office of Intelligence Research of the U.S. State Department had read the signs many years earlier. In a 1949 report analyzing the reasons why most Latin American countries failed "to establish stable and democratic systems," it pointed out that "the econonomic development of these countries, adapted to the shifting market of the industrial countries of the northern hemisphere and handicapped by a system of large landed estates, was so unbalanced as to prevent the emergence of an economically strong and politically conscious middle class."[2]

The message of this report might have been overlooked in the years immediately following its release. The economic model, although unbalanced, did achieve significant growth in the 1950s and 1960s. The then popular trickle-down theory persuaded many observers that the prosperity of the oligarchs would gradually permeate the entire society. That did not happen even when times were good. On the contrary, the poor were getting poorer as the rich were getting richer. And the onset in the late 1960s of a recession that still continues to deepen soon brought the discontent, the misery, and the revolutionary mood described by Kissinger. Current prognoses of the world economy indicate a steady shrinking for the foreseeable future. This, combined with a continued growth in population well into the next century, means that the extent and intensity of poverty will continue to grow unless world social structures are radically changed.

The bishops of Latin America had read the signs long before Kissinger did. At Medellín, Colombia, in 1968, they described as sinful the oppressive structures created and maintained by the local oligarchies and the international imperialism of money with which they were allied. They said that the striking poverty of so many people was the most decisive reality in the region, one that "cries out to heaven." They marvelled that the people had suffered such oppression in silence for so long and warned that a day of reckoning was not far away.

Offering the concept of a liberating God to replace the god of private property, they said: "Many parts of Latin America are experiencing a situation of injustice which can be called institutionalized violence. The structures of industry and agriculture, of the national and international economy, the cultural and political life all violate fundamental rights. Entire peoples lack the bare necessities and live in a condition of such dependency that they can exercise neither initiative nor responsibility.

Similarly, they lack all possibility of cultural improvement and of participation in social and political life. Such situations call for global, daring, urgent, and basically renewing change. It should surprise nobody that the temptation to violence should manifest itself in Latin America. It is wrong to abuse the patience of people who have endured for years a situation that would be intolerable if they were more aware of their rights as human beings."[3]

The overwhelming majority of the people of Central America, the impoverished victims of repression, agree with Mr. Kissinger and the Latin American bishops that the conditions in which they live are intolerable. The successful armed challenge to Somoza demonstrated this in Nicaragua. The popular forces in El Salvador would long since have achieved the same objective were it not for the massive military and economic aid poured into that country by the United States. Neither could the reactionary forces in Guatemala have maintained their reign of terror for so many years without U.S. aid given both directly and at various times through Israeli, Argentine, and Taiwanese surrogates. In Honduras, the long smoldering discontent is erupting more openly; and both there and in Costa Rica the objective conditions, if not quickly changed, can be expected to project the people along the path already taken by their neighbors.

Given this agreement on the ends that must be reached, namely, transformation of the conditions of life of the vast majority, the discussion narrows to means. What means are best calculated to reach the desired goal? Who should control the process?

Two radically different approaches are being tested since 1979, the year in which the Nicaraguan revolutionaries came to power and prodded an alarmed United States to take action to deal with a situation it had belatedly recognized as getting out of control. One is revolutionary, the other developmentalist.

Revolution implies change so rapid and radical as to involve the smashing of one system and the building of another on its ruins, what the bishops at Medellín called "global, daring, urgent, and basically renewing." In principle it need not involve violence. Historically, however, it always has. Structures of power do not peaceably accept their own destruction.

Central America has as yet only one model of revolution in place, that of Nicaragua. The FDR and FMLN, the political and military "vanguard" organizations of the popular movements in El Salvador, are on record as seeking to establish a similar system. The participatory structures they have created to promote health, education, and nutrition in the large part of the country they control confirm that they are in fact living up to their stated commitments. What forms would emerge in Guatemala from a revolution dominated by that country's Indians must remain a matter of speculation. One can only assume that they would be unlikely to look to Eastern Europe or China for a model if one is available next door.

The Nicaraguan model is eclectic and pragmatic. It takes its name from Augusto César Sandino who from 1927 to 1932 led a guerrilla campaign to liberate his country both from the U.S. army of occupation and the client regime Washington had imposed. His thought involves several basic principles. It is nationalist, not in a chauvinistic sense but in the positive sense that Nicaraguans are entitled to determine their own destiny and choose the form of government they believe best suited to their needs. It is committed to democracy. This does not mean the system, common in Latin America and elsewhere, that enables the elite groups which dominate the economy to maintain control while allowing the public to ratify their decisions from time to time. Rather it is a participatory system in which the people through their institutions play an active part in all decision making, a situation that is possible only when every citizen has the right to work and enjoys a level of education and access to information that enables him or her to make informed judgments on matters affecting personal and community life.

Miguel D'Escoto, the Maryknoll priest who is Nicaragua's Minister of Foreign Affairs since 1979, says that the great growth in the Sandinista Front in the 1970s was a direct result of the new social awareness among Catholics, especially the young, as a result of the commitment to the poor and to social justice taken by the bishops at Medellín in 1969. He quotes Daniel Ortega, now president, as having stated publicly that he went to the revolutionary struggle because he understood that was what was demanded of him if he was to be faithful to Christ.

D'Escoto also recognizes that the Sandinista thought is influenced by Marxism, as is all twentieth-century thinking. "The emphasis on conceptualizing the present as an historical trend to better understand it is one of the contributions of Marxism. From a philosophical perspective, of course, Marx helps us understand the connection between liberal thought, capitalism, and racism.... So in the Sandinistas, we have been very much aided by Marxist thought to understand some great problems. But we have been equally or more influenced by Christian thought."[4]

The electoral system established by law in 1983 is modeled after "key components of the French, Italian, Austrian, and Swedish electoral systems."[5] It includes proportional representation, a system that gives far greater representation in the legislature to minority parties than the U.S. or British single constituency, winner-take-all, method of election. The elections held in November 1984 were observed by official delegations covering a broad spectrum of world opinion. They included a delegation from the Latin American Studies Association of the United States, a body composed of the top Latin Americanists in U.S. colleges and universities, an official delegation from the Dutch government, an Irish Inter-Party Parliamentary Delegation, a British Parliamentary Delegation, and the Socialist International. Never had a Latin American election been so closely scrutinized. A national campaign during the previous year had registered 93.7 percent of the voting-age population, and although voting was not obligatory, 75 percent of those registered cast ballots. Six opposition parties, three to the right of the Sandinistas and three to the left, appeared on the ballot. The Sandinistas received 63 percent of the votes and won 61 of the 96 seats in the National Assembly. It was the consensus of the international observers that no major political tendency had been denied access to the electoral process, that no party had been prevented from carrying out an active campaign, and that the election was the cleanest held in Nicaragua since 1928.

In the restructuring of the economy, the Nicaraguan model has shown both creativity and pragmatism. Rejecting the various options provided by existing "socialist" regimes, it proposed a mixed economy with 60 to 70 percent in private hands, the remainder divided equally between state-owned enterprises and cooperatives. The private sector should, however, be subject to public control to the extent needed to direct the country's economic resources, as a top priority, into production designed to fulfill the basic needs of all citizens.

The specific reforms to implement this policy closely followed the recommendations being made since the 1960s by the UN Economic Commission for Latin America. The main elements were a land reform to correct gross disparities of wealth in the rural areas and to create a bigger internal market, and the nationalization of the banks and foreign trade to ensure that the export earnings did not end up in private bank accounts in the United States or Switzerland. These steps were facilitated by the fact that the assets of Somoza and his associates included a fifth of Nicaragua's cultivable land and a quarter of the industrial sector.

Jesuit economist Xabier Gorostiaga, a major architect of the Nicaraguan model, explains its originality. "Economists speak of the trickle-down effect by which growth and goods are first produced to satisfy the needs of the wealthy minority and then descend toward the lower sectors. The Sandinista revolution searches for a contrary dynamic, a trickle-up effect, starting from the bottom. It first satisfies basic needs and then raises the goods of the economy upward toward the middle sectors, eventually arriving at nonessential consumption and private accumulation, once the basic needs of the majority have been satisfied. These two concepts respond to different logics: the logic of private accumulation and the logic of the satisfaction of the needs of the majority, with the subsequent initiation of social accumulation and the development of productive forces calculated to overcome underdevelopment."[6]

This same thought is further developed, and from a different viewpoint, by another on-the-spot observer of the Nicaraguan experiment, liberation theologian Pablo Richard.

"For me, the essential thing about Nicaragua's revolutionary process is that it has succeeded in following what I call 'the logic of the majority.' This 'logic' is visible in three areas: First, in the revolution's defense of life—but life defined in the very concrete terms of basic needs, jobs, land, health, and education. I see a model of development evolving in which the overriding goal is to satisfy these needs and assure a dignified life in all its dimensions.

"Second, the 'logic of the majority' demands broad participation—and with my own eyes I've seen that going on in Nicaragua. Sure we can all wait around for the Internationaal Fund to satisfy our basic needs. But in Nicaragua the people themselves have organized to meet those needs. That's why to understand what's happening in Nicaragua, it's absolutely essential to understand this widespread participation. An organized conscious people is emerging and struggling for its rights. What we [theologians] describe as 'the historical project of the poor' is what is actually taking place in Nicaragua.

"Finally—and this is extremely important—a new consciousness is growing up in Nicaragua, a new dimension in human awareness. Essentially, this has happened through the participation of groups that tend to be pushed aside in other Latin American societies; I'm referring to indigenous people, blacks, women, and Christians.

"These three factors—satisfaction of basic needs through a new development model; broad participation; and the emergence of a new consciousness—seem to me to have great importance for the rest of Latin America and for all the Third World. From Latin America and from the Third World in general we see in Nicaragua a concrete model for development, a model it is actually possible to carry out. In this sense, Nicaragua has become a sort of reference point for grassroots movements throughout Latin America."[7]

The immediate impact of the application of this policy was spectacular. Between 1979 and 1983, in spite of the diversion of resources to defense against the mounting attacks of the U.S.-supported contras, Nicaragua maintained the highest rate of economic growth and the highest rate of investment of any country in Latin America. Simultaneously, major progress was made with another economic goal of the revolution, the internationalization of dependency. Under the Somozas, the United States had an effective monopoly on Nicaraguan trade, both import and export. A small country like Nicaragua with modest resources, says Gorostiaga, cannot hope to create an enclave. It has to export a significant part of its production in order to obtain goods and services it cannot itself generate. But it should not be dependent on a single supplier. The more diversified its trade, the more flexibility it has in its economic decisions.

The first years of the revolution also saw spectacular progress in health. Infant mortality fell from 120 to 70 deaths per 1,000 live births. Mass campaigns of immunization, malaria prophylaxis, and sanitation have brought a major decrease in the incidence of malaria, polio, and measles, and cut deaths from diarrhea significantly.

The literacy crusade of 1980, headed by Father Fernando Cardenal, cut illiteracy from 52 to 13 percent. Continuing education has ensured that the majority of the newly literate retained and built on their basic skills. The number of teachers has grown from 12,700 in 1978 to well over 50,000. Half of them are in adult education, a program unknown before 1980.

Land reform has moved through several phases. The 20 percent of the country's arable land seized from Somoza and his associates was converted in 1979 into state farms. Next, land purchased by the government was turned over to production cooperatives, a form of operation now preferred to state ownership because it has proved more productive. Next, farmers who had homesteaded in previously uninhabited areas in the interior received titles to their holdings. In 1985, several thousand peasant families were given individual holdings, much of the land being taken from state farms. By the end of that year, more than 120,000 families, the majority of all rural families in Nicaragua, had benefited, making this one of the most significant land reforms in Latin American history. It is the only land reform in Central America radical enough to break the link between the landed elite and political power. It is also unique in that expropriation was based, not on size, but on nonuse. Landowners could retain their entire property, no matter how extensive, as long as they kept it in production. They could lose it only if they left it idle or decapitalized it.

Political analysts in Nicaragua and elsewhere in Central America have told me that they see these achievements as explaining the popularity the revolution continues to enjoy. They suggest that this is why the contras choose health centers, schools, and cooperatives as preferred targets. This would be consonant with the analysis of informed observers (which I share) that the ultimate fear of decision makers in Washington is that the Nicaraguan model, if given a chance, would succeed; and that every country in the Third World would want to imitate it. That would create the nightmare situation projected by financier Bernard Baruch in a memorandum to President Franklin D. Roosevelt. If Mexico is allowed to nationalize U.S. property, Baruch wrote, every country in Latin America will follow suit and we will no longer control their natural resources nor be able to use them on terms we dictate.

President Reagan has obstinately refused to admit that the Sandinistas ever did anything right. He reportedly fired his first ambassador to Nicaragua, Anthony Quainton, for listing "the gains of the revolution" in his classified 1983 year-end summary and for stating publicly that the Nicaraguan government was not antisemitic. It is a matter of record that Quainton spoke freely to his friends about the significant success of the programs of land reform, health care, and education.

After 1983, however, intensification of the U.S.-backed contra war of sabotage brought about a negative rate of growth. Investment had to be drastically reduced, and health and education services were cut back. Defense and the supply of the basic food needs of the population became the top priorities.

Gorostiaga remains convinced, nevertheless, that were it not for the war being waged by the United States on many fronts, the Nicaragua model could work, at least for Nicaragua. "We have abundance of good land and other natural resources," he says. "Morale is high. Even suffering cannot shake it, as anyone can see. We made incredible progress until the contra war slowed it down. When that war ends, within two years we will again be raising the gross national product at a 10 percent rate, and we can continue this level of growth indefinitely."

I believe that the U.S. strategy is also designed to destroy the Nicaraguan model by radicalizing it. World opinion is sympathetic to a small country attempting social reform within a democratic framework and with the obvious support of the overwhelming majority of its people.

Washington hopes that the hardships inflicted on the civilian population will cause the people to blame the policies of their own government, forcing it to introduce totalitarian controls. If such is Washington's design, it is not working. Apart from any other evidence, we have the testimony of sixty thousand U.S. citizens who since 1979 have gone to see for themselves, many of them living and working for considerable periods in Nicaragua. At any given moment, 1,500 to 3,000 are scattered around the country, in direct contact with Nicaraguan civilians as agronomists, forest managers, teachers, doctors, nurses, Catholic or Protestant pastoral agents, laboratory technicians, translators, documenters of violations of human rights. A faith commitment, Catholic, Protestant, or Jewish, motivates the vast majority. These eyewitnesses testify to the readiness of the peasants to defend their homes and the revolution against the contras. The peasants, they say, point to U.S. policy, not that of their own government, as the cause of the extreme hardships they are enduring. No other Latin American country places in the hands of the poor weapons they could use to overthrow their own government.

Their testimony is more than a consensus. It is virtually unanimous. They agree that mistakes have been committed, that human rights have been violated. But they deny that there is an official policy of repression or a secret totalitarian agenda distinct from the agenda formulated before the Triumph and frequently reaffirmed. The abuses are those that occur in every country defending itself from a mortal threat to its survival.

Americas Watch and other human rights organizations, for example, have documented mistreatment of the Miskito Indians of Nicaragua's Atlantic Coast during 1981 and 1982. When challenged, the Sandinistas publicly admitted their mistakes and in particular their failure to recognize adequately the different cultural background of the Atlantic Coast. After extended negotiations with representatives of the various groups on the Atlantic Coast, the National Assembly in September 1987 enacted a law guaranteeing the political, economic, linguistic, cultural, and religious rights of indigenous peoples, and establishing autonomous governments for the Indian and Creole communities of the Atlantic Coast. Nicaragua is the first American country to have such a law. Recent Americas Watch reports confirm that no officially sanctioned violations of the human rights of the Miskitos continue, and they specifically criticize the Reagan administration's "unabashed use of half-truths and of outright lies" in their efforts to discredit the Nicaraguan government. The treatment of the Miskitos by the Sandinistas at a time when many of them were cooperating with the contras has been remarkably more humane than the U.S. treatment of its Nisei citizens in World War II.[8]

Dr. Richard Shaull, for many years a Presbyterian fraternal worker in Colombia and Brazil, and later a professor of theology at Princeton Divinity School, has been observing the Nicaraguan revolution for the past several years. His conclusions are striking.

"One of the reasons why so many North Americans who travel to Nicaragua return with a positive attitude toward that country is that they have seen the sacrificial outpouring of life by women and men committed to offering a new life of opportunity to the poor. On my first visit there after the victory of the revolution, that is what most caught my attention. As a result of my living and traveling in Central and South America over many years, I had come to realize that poverty can be overcome, if at all, only by an almost superhuman effort on the part of large numbers of people throughout society. In Nicaragua I saw this happening. I met individuals and teams in the ministries of housing and education and the program of land reform who had a clear vision of what they could do to serve the people, were committed to it, and were working very hard at low salaries to achieve their goals. They were joined by many others in intermediate positions who were equally committed to building a new society as they participated, often as volunteers, in programs of adult education, preventive medicine, and health care, the development of farm cooperatives."[9]

Such is the revolutionary model as Nicaragua has been applying it since 1979. During these same years, the United States has been promoting for Central America its developmentalist model, an updated version of the Alliance for Progress launched in the early 1960s as a response to the threat perceived to U.S. interests in Cuba's escape under Fidel Castro from U.S. economic domination. Since the failed attempt to overthrow Castro at the Bay of Pigs in 1961 and the Missile Crisis the following year, anticommunism has been the central doctrine of U.S. policy in Latin America and the Caribbean and its overriding goal has been to avoid "another Cuba." The policy has been supported by Democratic and Republican administrations alike. It led to the invasion of the Dominican Republic in 1965, the support of counterinsurgency warfare in Guatemala and elsewhere in the 1960s and 1970s, the destabilization of the Allende regime in Chile between 1970 and 1973, the response to the Sandinista victory in Nicaragua in 1979, the subsequent U.S. involvement in El Salvador, and the 1983 invasion of Grenada.

Communism is the enemy, but communism is never defined, nor is it ever pointed out that no such system exists anywhere in the world, whether understood as holding all things in common as some early Christians did, or in the sense proposed by Karl Marx of "from each according to ability and to each according to need." Rather we have a vague ideological catch-all that assumes a worldwide conspiracy controlled and manipulated by the Soviet Union with the objective of undermining and corrupting "the free world," which is to say, those nations that accept the leadership of the United States and are committed to defend free enterprise at all costs. One of the paradoxes is that, while it is gratuitously assumed that communism is a less human and less efficient system than capitalism, it has an extraordinary ability to impose itself. If a government allows a single communist to rise to a position of authority, it is only a matter of time until the entire apparatus of government is taken over by communists. Another peculiarity is that communists are always controlled from outside the country in which they operate, and ultimately from the Soviet Union. In the final analysis, this irrational anticommunism is a modern version of the Manichean heresy which posited a principle of evil in the world in conflict with the principle of good. Nothing less explains President Reagan's characterization of the Soviet Union as the empire of evil.

This emotional fixation goes back to the late 1940s when the Soviet Union developed the nuclear bomb and emerged as a challenger to U.S. world hegemony, and it has been used ever since to justify U.S. support of rightwing dictatorships. Already in 1950, George Kennan, then the State Department's expert on Soviet Affairs, flew to Rio de Janeiro to tell U.S. ambassadors in Latin America that they should not be upset when the government to which they were accredited engaged in police repression of their own citizens. "This is not shameful since the communists essentially are traitors," Kennan said. "It is better to have a strong regime in power than a liberal government if it is indulgent and relaxed and penetrated by communists."

The Rockefeller Report of 1969 plays on the same themes. Communist subversion, it says, "is a reality today with alarming potential," and "the subversive capabilities of these communist forces are increasing throughout the hemisphere." Political forces which seek to end stagnation, poverty, and oppression are "enemies"; they are the "covert forces of communism," who "exploit" such factors. "Clearly, the opinion in the United States that communism is no longer a serious factor in the western hemisphere is thoroughly wrong.... Forces of anarchy, terror, and subversion are loose in the Americas."

Kennan's policy and that of subsequent U.S. administrations was one of containment. It sought to prevent the spread of socialist regimes. The Reagan administration has made significant changes. Earlier, the policy was pursued by a variety of means, with military force as a last resort. Since 1980, however, the principal effort of U.S. policy has been to build up the military forces of countries which it identifies as targets of communist aggression, providing the armaments, the training, and even the supervision of military operations, as in El Salvador. A 1985 congressional report on aid to El Salvador revealed a tenfold increase from 1980 to 1984, with war-related aid constituting 74 percent of the total. For fiscal year 1988, U.S. aid was greater than the entire Salvadoran budget, $608 million from the United States and $582 million from domestic revenues.

The fixation on Central America, primarily because of Nicaragua, has meant that more than half of all U.S. aid to Latin America since 1980 has been concentrated in Costa Rica, Honduras, and El Salvador, three small countries with less than 4 percent of the population of Latin America. Nor do the official aid figures tell the whole story. The aid is directed mostly to building up the armed forces which traditionally identify with the reactionary elements in each country and block democratic openings. The actual cost of this policy to the United States is much greater than the direct aid.

In 1985, for example, the cost of naval and ground exercises, military construction, and U.S. personnel located in Central America, was considerably more than twice the cost of aid.

Shortly after President Reagan's inauguration in 1981, the Administration came up with a highly trumpeted solution for the ills of the entire region. Called the Caribbean Basin Initiative (CBI) it promised to revitalize "friendly" Central American and Caribbean countries through a $350 million aid package and a radical application of free-market principles. Latin Americans, said the President, should "make use of the magic of the marketplace, the market of the Americas." If equitably distributed, the $30 million would have done no more than slow the capital outflow. Actually, nearly half of the total went to El Salvador. The impact on the rest of the region was negligible, and little more was heard about the CBI after the 1983 lightning visit of the Kissinger Commission to Central America.

The Commission called for a $400 million "emergency stabilization program," to include substantially increased military assistance to El Salvador, Honduras, and Guatemala. The Commission took for granted that the United States would continue to fund the contras, describing their attacks on Nicaragua as an "incentive" to negotiate, nowhere raising any question as to the legitimacy of such funding under international law and U.S. treaty obligations. The emergency stabilization program, it said, should be followed by an $8 billion 5-year aid program with unprecedented U.S. involvement in and responsibility for the economies of Central America. Implementation of these recommendations would formally establish a neocolonial relationship at least as onerous as the Soviet controls over the economies of its Eastern European satellites.

The first element in the Kissinger program, the expansion of the Central American armies and their training in sophisticated counterinsurgency techniques, was following an old script, the one that had succeeded in Nicaragua when in 1933 the United States handed over control to the first Somoza, having built up the National Guard to enable him to keep the people in their place. It had already succeeded in El Salvador the previous year (1932), when the army, with U.S. approval, massacred an estimated thirty thousand peasant leaders and potential leaders, ushering in forty years of "the peace of the cemetery."

Even before Kissinger's encouragement, the armies—ably assisted by Death Squads—had been busy. In Guatemala, the army and its allies have committed fifty thousand political murders in a decade and turned more than a million Indians and peasants into refugees. The score in El Salvador has been approximately the same. Honduras is far behind, with political assassinations in the low hundreds, but death squads remain active and a consistent pattern of human rights violations continues.

Costa Rica, without an army since 1949, has no organized guerrilla movement. Its economy, however, has deteriorated seriously over the past two decades, and it has limped along by means of massive borrowing. Today, it has the highest per-capita debt of any nation other than the United States and Israel. The United States, anxious to involve it in its harassment of Nicaragua, has persuaded it to accept arms and training that have effectively converted its Rural and Civil Guards into counterinsurgency armed forces, the strength of which has more than doubled to ten thousand effectives in eight years.

All of this expansion of the armed forces of Central America, including the contras, is designed to implement U.S. foreign policy goals. These goals, established in principle by President Monroe in 1823, have been steadily broadened as U.S. military, economic, and diplomatic control of the region grew. Their most recent formulation came from President Reagan when he told Congress, 1 May 1985, that he had declared a national emergency on the ground that "the policies and actions of the government of Nicaragua constitute an unusual and extraordinary threat to the national security and foreign policy of the United States." His message was that the United States has the right to intervene if any nation pursues policies—or has a form of government—that the United States unilaterally decides to be a threat to its interests. An almost identical formulation had been offered by Assistant-Secretary of State Edward Miller in 1950, eighteen years before the Soviets in the Brezhnev Doctrine made a similar assertion of their right to intervene in the internal affairs of their satellites.

The growth in size, firepower, and professionalism of the Central American armies has been accompanied by an ideological assimilation of the Doctrine of National Security. This Doctrine, which inspired the short-lived tyrannical military dictatorships in Argentina and Brazil and which still inspires the waning dictatorship of General Pinochet in Chile, asserts that the army is the exclusive judge of what is good for the nation. The armed forces have consequently replaced the oligarchies as the controllers and manipulators of the economy and the society, a status of privilege that they understand they enjoy as long as they implement political and economic policies determined by the United States. The recent substitution of civilian presidents for military dictators in Guatemala, El Salvador, and Honduras has not changed the reality. Ultimate power still stays with the armed forces. The civilian regimes exist at the will of the military which determine the parameters within which they can function.

As a result of the Inter-American Mutual Defense Treaty signed at Rio de Janeiro in 1947, all the armies of Latin America have been standardized in the U.S. pattern, with U.S. equipment and training, but with one important difference. The Special Action Force for Latin America, better known as the Green Berets, was formed in 1962 and located at Fort Gulick in the Panama Canal Zone, which since that time has been the most important center of training of Latin American army officers. Most of its courses deal with military civic action and counterinsurgency. Its Irregular Warfare Committee "teaches various measures required to defeat an insurgent' [movement] on the battlefield, as well as military civic action functions in an insurgent environment."[10] The Green Berets in addition to providing the tone and distinctive character of the training at Fort Gulick, both ideological and technical, have sent mobile training teams to work with every Latin American army except those of Cuba, Haiti, and Mexico. In consequence, the Latin American armed forces everywhere have internalized the attitudes of this special force rather than those of the peacetime armed forces of the United States. The difference is critical. The Green Berets have never seen themselves as part of the regular army, but as a group with its own purposes and methods.

Organized in 1952 as a revival of the World War II OSS (precursor of the CIA) to fight the Cold War in Europe, the force was heavily European in its composition, men who had been uprooted and forced to choose exile when the Soviet Union occupied their homelands. A one-time member has described them as "self-consciously uprooted men, emotionally and intellectually detached from the mainstream of civilian society." What was most striking about them, he said, was their ability to kill, without passion or the justifications of panic or crisis, anyone who presented an obstacle to the orderly conduct of an intelligence operation. "Such a clerkly impersonality about killing a prisoner has found a comparison in the administrative routine of the Nazi death camps, whose SS commanders would complain to each other about the bureaucratic difficulties of their task and compare notes on the technical and organizational solutions they found most satisfactory."[11] Inside reports on the "administrative processes" used over the past decade by the armed forces of Guatemala, El Salvador, and Honduras show that they have fully internalized the values taught them by the Green Berets.

The reason offered by Henry Kissinger for building up the armed forces of Central America, a reason regularly repeated by President Reagan and his advisers, is that the Soviet Union has manipulated the popular dissatisfaction. "The Soviet Union threat is real," said the Kissinger Report, because "the conditions that invite revolution... have been exploited by hostile forces." This is "a Soviet-Cuban thrust to make Central America part of the geostrategic challenge." The underlying assumption is that the region is so volatile and unstable, and the Soviet Union so aggressive and wily, that sooner or later our enemies will gain a foothold on the American land mass, threatening the Panama Canal to the south, and to the north first Mexico and eventually the United States itself.

El Salvador and Nicaragua are the two countries in which the validity of these assumptions is most clearly being put to the test. Their logic demands that the armed insurgency in El Salvador and the revolutionary government in Nicaragua both lack significant popular support and will collapse once the "exploitation by hostile forces" is frustrated. How does this "doctrinal position," as Senator Daniel Moynihan has characterized it, stand up to the experience of the eight years during which it has dictated U.S. policy toward these two countries?

The United States has spent several billion dollars since 1980 in trying to substitute its project for that of the popular forces. The Salvadoran army and security forces have grown from 13,250 effectives in 1980 to 55,000 in 1987. Other security forces and such paramilitary units as ORDEN raise the total troop strength to 110,000. The United States has supplied dozens of helicopters and several kinds of ground-attack aircraft, including the AC-47 gunships. By 1983 it was clear that this army was losing to the popular forces, and since that time the United States has taken over the management of the war. It has reorganized the command structure and its "advisers," aided by continuous U.S. air reconaissance, not only dictate strategy but direct field operations. Ground and air attacks on civilians constitute a basic element in strategy, the objective being to force peasants to flee contested zones, thus depriving the popular forces of their support structure. This policy constitutes a de facto recognition that the popular forces have the overwhelming sympathy of the civilian population.

The war has resulted in more than 60,000 deaths in a population of 5 million, considerably more than a million refugees and displaced persons, and damage to homes, crops, and infrastructure in excess of $1 billion. U.S. involvement has prevented the collapse of the regime, but the cost has been enormous. Most of the aid has been consumed by the military. The rest has gone to economic projects that benefit almost exclusively the U.S.-based transnational corporations and their local associates in the oligarchy. But the promised economic expansion has not followed. Instead, domestic capital investment has ceased, the money flowing instead to Swiss bank accounts. The military stalemate is projected to continue for as long as the United States maintains its present policies.

Surveillance satellites and U.S. spy planes based in Panama and Honduras have for all these years kept unceasing watch on everything that enters or leaves without producing the evidence that either Russia or Cuba is providing the arms and supplies used by the popular forces. Instead, it is well established that a major part of these arms and supplies flow to them from the United States through the Salvadoran army, being captured in battle or ambush, bought from corrupt army officers, or brought by deserters. It is significant that the FMLN has never had sophisticated anti-aircraft weapons, although they desperately need them to counter the incessant air bombardments. This is the one weapon the United States does not supply to the Salvadoran army which does not need it because the FMLN has no aircraft.

In the early 1980s, the FDR and FMLN, the political and military organizations of the popular movements, believed they could achieve a military victory in the same way as Nicaragua had. Since about 1983, however, they have decided that this is not possible. No matter how much they increased their armed strength, the United States was able and willing to counter with ever more advanced weapons of destruction to the other side. In consequence, their strategy changed to one of maintaining a stalemate that would finally force the oligarchy to agree to a political resolution. Indeed, their political analysts have now gone a step further. Even if the opportunity developed to crush the Salvadoran armed forces, they would not take it. The collapsing army, they believe, would request and be given direct U.S. air and ground support. Their conclusion is that the only viable way is that of negotiations.

The people of El Salvador, even though prepared to support the FMLN for as long as it takes to change the system, are understandably tired of a war that has left no family without a victim and forced one Salvadoran in five into city slums or exile. President Duarte is on record as favoring dialogue, with Archbishop Rivera Damas ready and anxious to serve as impartial go-between. But here we are faced with the fact that the façade of democracy which Washington has created as a front for its intervention, lacks all substance. The Reagan administration is committed to a military solution. The armed forces, in which it has vested real power, block every initiative that could lead to serious negotiations.

Both sides agree that the war is stalemated. The FMLN has learned to adjust to each change in the strategy of the armed forces. When in 1980 and 1981 the army concentrated its forces in the capital, it moved its offensives to the countryside. Later, it changed from large concentrations involved in semi-conventional warfare to small units dispersed all over the country. When the armed forces, combining air attacks and ground sweeps, drove much of the civilian population from the countryside to city slums in order to deprive the guerrilla units of their logistical base, they followed the people into the slums and renewed urban attacks. At the same time, they retained their bases in the countryside. Several times during 1987 they launched successful, large-scale attacks on major army bases and conducted a war of attrition in all fourteen of the country's departments that continues to take a heavy toll of army casualties.

The stalemate can be expected to continue indefinitely. Edwin Corr, U.S. ambassador in El Salvador, estimates that it will take eight years of U.S. support to enable the armed forces to bring the war to a successful conclusion. But he adds an important condition. It can be done in this time only if the U.S. Congress gives a green light to the administration to plan for the long term instead of having to beg for money each year. Since the principal congressional questioning at budget time has had to do with violations of human rights, it would follow that what the administration wants is a free hand to use whatever means are necessary. Guatemala between 1980 and 1983 inflicted a decisive defeat on its guerrillas, one from which they are only now recovering, by scorched earth policies of unbelievable barbarity against the civilian supporters. Nothing less could break the stalemate in El Salvador in favor of the armed forces.

The inference from what Corr is saying is that the U.S. administration would embark on an all-out scorched earth campaign in El Salvador, if given a free hand by Congress. All the elements are in place for such a campaign. After Duarte's election to the presidency the death squads lowered their profile significantly but they were not disbanded and the second half of 1987 was marked by a renewal of their activity. Speaking in his cathedral in January 1988, Archbishop Rivera Damas called for an end to these practices, saying that the death squads were continuing to torture and kill Salvadorans throughout the country.

The ability to implement such a scenario exists, but there are many reasons to think it will not occur. Especially after the Iran-Contragate fiasco, Congress is unlikely to give the administration the free hand it asks. Moreover, the project contains a self-defeating contradiction. It can break a movement for a time, as it did in Guatemala, but it cannot destroy it. Already in Guatemala the guerrilla movements have reconsolidated and are becoming steadily more active. In addition, Corr and other administration spokespersons refer frequently to Malaya as proof that a successful counterinsurgency war is possible. Sir Robert Thompson, however, who led the British forces in that 13-year conflict, is very specific about the conditions that must be met. In the first place he insists that the armed forces must "function in accord with the law." He also describes as "an absolutely fatal error" the giving of political and administrative authority to the military commanders. What he is saying is that a successful counterinsurgency must win the minds and hearts of the people. The U.S. project in El Salvador can only increase their alienation.

The FDR-FMLN similarly foresee an indefinite continuation of the war which in their view can end only when the United States abandons its insistence on a military solution and agrees to a political settlement. The people, although tired from the enormous suffering endured for so many years, remain determined to continue their support. Too much blood has been shed, they say. Such is the conclusion I have reached from talking to all kinds of people, political analysts, members of base communities in city slums, peasants in refugee camps, and others who have gone back to the countryside in resettlement programs, and noncombatant sympathizers in FMLN-controlled territory in Morazán. In the struggle for minds and hearts, the armed forces do not seem to be making headway. They understand bullets but not beans.

The claim by the U.S. government that it is entitled to determine what the people of Nicaragua want has escalated fantasy to even greater heights than has the same pretension in El Salvador. It has forced Washington to reject the evidence accepted by every other nation in the world that the government that now rules that country is there by the free choice of its people, a choice confirmed in blood to establish it and reconfirmed in the blood shed to maintain it against the contras.

Whether or not the Nicaraguan government has grossly violated the human rights of many of its citizens is not the issue here. Whether or not it seeks to impose a Marxist-Leninist dictatorship and—in President Reagan's words—create "a totalitarian dungeon" is equally beside the point, although the evidence of creditworthy observers given earlier establishes that such is not the case. What is relevant is that the U.S. administration not only asserts the right to interfere unilaterally in the internal affairs of a sovereign state with which it maintains diplomatic relations but pursues courses of action it does not dare announce publicly and engages in crude deception in its efforts to hide what it is doing from its own citizens and their elected representatives.

The results of this U.S. policy include 43,176 casualties between 1980 and mid-1987, 22,495 dead, 12,065 wounded, and 8,616 kidnapped or captured. The corresponding figures for the United States, with a population of 240 million, would be more than three million casualties, half of which would be fatal. The fatalities would exceed the total number of U.S. citizens killed in World War I, World War II, the Korean War, and Vietnam. Direct losses caused by the war in 1986 alone, including destruction by the contras of productive facilities, was $275 million, $45 million more than Nicaragua's export earnings for the year.

The extent to which the U.S. administration is ready to go to return Nicaragua to satellite status was highlighted by the scandal over illegal arms sales profits to the contras that broke in November 1986, as well as blatant and finally admitted deception of the Congress itself. The subsequent congressional hearings, while leaving many questions unanswered, clearly established a long history of double-dealing and involvement in and with international terrorism. Such deception was necessary because the administration was determined to pursue policies that have been rejected by majorities in every poll of U.S. public opinion since 1980. Thus, congressional funding for the contras was originally obtained on the ground that the contra army was needed to block the flow of arms from the Sandinistas to the popular forces in El Salvador. The "evidence" presented to support this claim was so flimsy that even the *Wall Street Journal* rejected it. David MacMichael, a contract analyst for the CIA from 1981 to 1983, was one of a very small group of people with a security clearance that allowed him to see all intelligence and cable traffic from Central America. He resigned in protest against the distorted use of his analyses to prove that the insurgency in El Salvador was supported and controlled by the Sandinistas. "The Reagan hardliners," he wrote in the *New York Times*, "have succeeded in silencing most of those in the State Department, the military, the intelligence agencies, and elsewhere who doubted the information on which this policy was based. The silencing of dissent has been the administration's only Central American policy success."

In December 1982, disturbed by growing evidence of the administration's commitment to underwrite the contras in their openly declared intentions to overthrow the government of Nicaragua, Congress passed the Boland amendment which prohibited the use by the CIA or the Defence Department of any funds voted by Congress for "military equipment, military training or advice, or other support of military activities... for the purpose of overthrowing the government of Nicaragua." For the two and a half years in which the amendment was in force, the administration continued to fund the contras, sinking ever deeper into the underworld of intrigue and collaboration with terrorists exposed in the Iran-Contra hearings. The 1986 decision of the World Court details the many attempts to destroy Nicaragua's economy and overthrow its government. The Court found that the U.S. "financial support, backing, supply of weapons, intelligence, and logistical support" to the contras "constitutes a clear breach of the principle of nonintervention." These actions involved not only disregard for the basic principles of customary international law but specific violations of the Geneva Convention and the charters of the United Nations and the Organization of the American States. The UN Charter states: "All members shall settle their international disputes by peaceful means" and refrain from "the threat or use of force against the territorial integrity or political independence of any state." The OAS Charter is even stronger, forbidding not only armed force but "any other form of interference or attempted interference."

The UN Charter further provides that members who fail to resolve disputes by direct negotiations may ask the Security Council to rule on the issues. Nicaragua took this route in protest against the contra and CIA attacks, which included the mining of its harbors. The United States was able to avoid condemnation only by exercising its veto. Similarly, when the World Court's ruling roundly condemned the United States, it took the unprecedented action of "temporarily" excluding disputes involving any of the countries of Central America from its 1946 pledge to accept the court's jurisdiction.

It would be easy, but not accurate, to place all the blame on the Reagan administration. What in fact it has done is to build on a process initiated by its predecessor. In the months immediately following the ouster of Somoza in July 1979 it was uncertain if the new regime would in fact carry out its promises of a radical social revolution. Many regimes had come to power in Central America on the basis of promises that were quickly forgotten. But Washington, obsessed with the idea that major social change anywhere benefits the Soviet Union and harms the United States, was taking no chances. Before Somoza fell, the CIA was already jockeying for position. Anticipating Somoza's overthrow, President Carter in 1978 had authorized CIA aid for "democratic elements" in Nicaraguan society. The very day Somoza fled, the CIA began—under Red Cross camouflage—to ferry officers and men of the National Guard from Nicaragua and from Honduras—to which many had fled—to Miami. Soon training as a counterrevolutionary force would begin in Florida where winking at the Neutrality Act is a way of life. Argentina, then a military dictatorship with close ties to the United States, took over training and assistance for the contras in 1980, so that Washington could keep a low profile, an arrangement that continued until Argentina lost the support of the United States in the Falkland-Malvinas war.

Also in 1980, armed attacks by the contras began from bases in Honduras, a fact that President Reagan conveniently overlooked when he said the Sandinista military build-up began two and a half years before the U.S.-backed rebels took up arms. In fact, it was not until many months after the contra attacks began that Nicaragua received its first shipments of heavy Soviet-made arms. And two white papers issued or revised by the U.S. Departments of State and Defense in 1985 show that Soviet-bloc military supplies to Nicaragua were not significant until 1982.[12] Deliveries in that and the following years consisted mainly of defensive weaponry, such as antiaircraft guns and missiles and weapons useful for operations against the contras. Even in late 1985, Nicaragua reportedly had fewer than thirty combat aircraft, none of them supersonic, including not more than fifteen Soviet Hind helicopter gunships. El Salvador, by contrast, reportedly had forty U.S. Huey gunships along with some four dozen A-37 jet fighters or fighterbombers. Honduras also was far better equipped in air power than Nicaragua, even without taking into account the massive U.S. air presence in that country. It has long had French supersonic Mystères, and it is now receiving U.S. supersonic F-16s.[13] In November 1980, after more than a year of debate, Congress voted $75 million aid for Nicaragua. Sixty million was earmarked for projects designed to strengthen the big business elements opposed to the Sandinista revolutionary project, and this $60 million was disbursed. The balance, designated for the Nicaraguan government, was not.

While initiating a low level of coercion, the Carter administration hoped it could achieve the objectives of U.S. policy primarily by cooptation. The Reagan administration concentrated from the outset on coercion, its objective—though not publicly admitted until 1985—being "to remove... the present structure" of the Nicaraguan government.

After eight years, the effect in all of Central America of the U.S. project of cooptation and coercion is fully visible. Façade democracies have been installed in Guatemala, El Salvador, and Honduras, civilian administrations having been created by means of elections from which candidates representing the majority of the people were excluded. The parallel cancerous growth of the armed forces in these countries has destroyed any base on which democracy could be built. Instead, decision making has passed to army officers who are busy substituting themselves for the oligarchy as the principal beneficiaries of the corrupt political system. These countries are still in reality military dictatorships behind the façade of democracy.

On top of the deterioration resulting from the drop in demand and prices for the region's export crops, the ongoing war has wreaked untold suffering on the poor majority. A fourth of Salvadorans have lost their homes and their few belongings. The proportion of displaced Guatemalans is not much lower, and their treatment has been and continues to be even more brutal at the hands of armed forces and death squads. For several years, the armed forces have been rounding up refugees in Guatemala, the survivors of earlier massacres, and herding them into "model villages," the strategic hamlets of the Vietnam war. There they are held under military supervision, subject to indoctrination designed to destroy their culture and make them available as a captive labor force to exploit the agricultural and mineral resources of areas now being opened up. In both El Salvador and Guatemala much of the planning and financing of these projects comes from USAID.

The U.S. project has had an equally devastating impact on Nicaragua. All U.S. aid was cut off in 1981, including a promised and much-needed shipment of wheat, and trade was embargoed in 1985. Loans in the World Bank and the Inter-American Development Bank have been blocked. These actions, combined with economic sabotage by the CIA and the contras, have left the economy in tatters. The Nicaraguan government estimates the losses caused by the contra war at $3 billion. In September 1987, Nicaragua's Minister of Education, Fernando Cardenal, wrote U.S. Secretary of Education William Bennett to tell him that 411 teachers had been killed and 66 kidnapped; 59 students had been kidnapped; 46 schools had been destroyed and another 21 damaged, while 555 were temporarily closed, leaving 45,000 students without classrooms, and 480 adult centers were also closed. A quarter of a million peasants have been forced to leave their homes. More than half the national budget is consumed in defending the country against actual attacks and in preparation for the long threatened U.S. invasion.

In El Salvador a few months ago I talked to a world renowned theologian, Jon Sobrino, a man deeply committed to peace with justice. We touched on one of his favorite subjects, one on which he has expatiated to me several times over the years. It provides a perspective into which to place the issues described in this chapter.

In Central America, Sobrino says, we have two options, and only two. We have to choose life or choose death. Now, if we compare the two models for the future of Central America offered by revolutionary Nicaragua and by the U.S.-devised project to protect the privileges of the few at the expense of the many, is there any question as to which is a model of life, a model for hope for life for the people, and which a model of death, a model of torture, of oppression, of trampling on human rights and the rule of law? As Sobrino says, we must choose: choose death or choose life.

Notes

1. New York: Macmillan, 1984, Chapter 3.

2. OIR Report # 4780. 1 October 1949, p. 5.

3. *Documentos finales de Medellin*. Buenos Aires: Ediciones Paulinas, 1969, p. 50. Author's translation.

4. Dolly Pomerleau and Maureen Fiedler, eds., *Nicaragua: A Look at the Reality*. Washington, D.C.: Quixote Center, 1986 revised edition, p. 3.

5. Latin American Studies Association (LASA), *The Electoral Process in Nicaragua: Domestic and International Influences*. Report of the Latin American Studies Association Delegation to Observe the Nicaraguan General Election of November 4, 1984. Austin, Tex.: LASA 1984, p. 29.

6. Personal communication to author.

7. *Amanecer*, April 1987, Managua, Nicaragua. Author's translation.

8. Americas Watch, *The Miskitos in Nicaragua*, 1981-1984. New York: Americas Watch Committee, November 1984, p. 57. Conclusions reaffirmed in subsequent Americas Watch reports through 1987.

9. Richard Shaull, *Naming the Idols*. Yorktown Heights, N.Y.: Myer-Stone Books, 1988, p. 44.

10. Information supplied to author by Public Relations Office of U.S. South Command, Panama Canal Zone.

11. William Pfaff, in *Commentary*, New York, January 1970. For a fuller discussion of this theme, see Gary MacEoin, *Revolution Next Door: Latin America in the 1970s*. New York: Holt, Rinehart and Winston, 1971, pp. 141 ff.

12, Joel Brinkley, in *New York Times*, 30 March 1985; Thomas W. Walker, ed., *Reagan Versus the Sandinistas*. Boulder, Colorado: Westview Press, 1987, p. 174.

13. *Ibid.*

6.

Latin America Opts for Peace

On a Sunday evening in March 1986 President Reagan, in a televised address, told the nation why it was essential that Congress renew aid to the contras. The Sandinistas, he said, were "a communist organization,... the communist government of Nicaragua." They oppress their own people and subvert their neighbors. They are allies of the Soviets, obedient to their "Soviet mentors." As the president spoke, a map of Latin America progressively turned red as the "cancer" spread from country to country of the hemisphere. With the cancer came drug smuggling and "Latin peoples by the millions" streaming north to overrun the United States.

Nicaraguan state television carried the transmission in its entirety, correctly assuming that its distortion of reality would hurt both Mr. Reagan and his supporters inside Nicaragua. But it was not only Nicaraguans who were not convinced by the Reagan rhetoric. This and similar speeches and the policies they sought to justify have so deeply offended all Latin Americans as to create an unprecedented coalition. They have emotionally isolated the United States in the hemisphere more than ever before.

Most Latin American governments are unsympathetic to the revolutionary regime in Nicaragua. Their identification is not with the underprivileged majority of their own citizens but with the narrow stratum of wealth and privilege at the top. Nicaragua is a daily challenge, if not to their consciences, to their interests. Nevertheless, they have made it increasingly clear over the past several years that Nicaragua is a problem with which they are prepared to live, while the U.S. project to destroy that regime by means of its army of mercenaries is unacceptable to them.

Carlos Fuentes, distinguished Mexican statesman and world-renowned literary figure, who is currently a professor at the University of Cambridge (England), explains the rationale behind this paradox. "A Latin American government may deplore the Sandinistas, but it is bound to deplore—even more—U.S. intervention and arming bands against any constituted government in Latin America.

"Who can tell, given this president, when the same tactics will be used against Mexico, or Peru, or Colombia? Memories are short in the United States. They are long in Latin America. We remember the mutilation of Mexico in 1847 and of Colombia in 1901; the string of Marine landings in the Caribbean; the coups against Guatemala in 1954 and Chile in 1973, where elected governments were overthrown with the full connivance of U.S. administrations. Since the early twentieth century, Latin America has patiently attempted to construct an edifice of legal obligations with the United States in order to reduce the asymmetry of power in the hemisphere and construct a new relationship based on mutual respect and cooperation, not on dominance. But Reagan has shown us that the use of force and disregard for the law in dealing with Latin America are not things of the past. Past U.S. contempt for Latin America is thus compounded in the present."[1]

This historical perspective provided by Carlos Fuentes helps us to understand the growth of Latin American solidarity against the U.S. commitment to pursue a military solution of the various conflicts in Central America, including the ousting of Nicaragua's revolutionary government. The first formal steps were taken by Central America's immediate neighbors, those already affected or threatened by the militarization and the disruption of the social fabric. In September 1982, Mexico and Panama, alarmed by the turmoil in Central America, called on Honduras and Nicaragua, and also on the United States and Nicaragua, to initiate bilateral discussions as a way to reduce tension. Nicaragua agreed, but the United States refused and also persuaded Honduras to refuse.

The following January, representatives of Mexico, Panama, Colombia, and Venezuela met on Contadora Island, off the Pacific coast of Panama, and repeated the call for a negotiated settlement. A year later, Brazil, Peru, Argentina, and Uruguay formed a Support Group to promote the Contadora initiative. About the same time, the United States finally agreed to direct negotiations with Nicaragua but after several sessions terminated the talks in January 1985. The reason for the termination became clear a month later when President Reagan in a major address finally revealed that for him the only solution was the elimination of the revolutionary government and its reform program.

The Contadora Group produced a draft treaty to be signed by all five Central American nations. It would end support for irregular forces in the region, prohibit the use of one country as a base for guerrilla warfare against a neighboring country, prohibit foreign military bases in the region, and establish verification procedures, including on-site inspection. These years, 1983 and 1984, were marked by an enormous intensification of the U.S.-directed contra war against the economic infrastructure of Nicaragua. It included attacks on oil storage tanks and the mining of harbors carried out directly by CIA operatives, attacks for which the contras—on U.S. instructions—claimed credit at the time. Simultaneously, the United States tried to use the draft treaty to embarrass Nicaragua which had expressed objections to some of its clauses. In mid-September 1984, at a meeting of the European Economic Community (EEC) in San José, Costa Rica, Secretary of State George Shultz telegraphed every European foreign minister at the meeting urging them to deny all economic aid to Nicaragua "because of its refusal to sign the Contadora peace agreement." To Shultz's chagrin, before the telegrams reached Costa Rica, Nicaragua had announced it was ready to sign, saying its reservations did not justify a continuation of conflict in the region.

Faced with this new situation, Washington immediately engaged in a flurry of negotiations with the other Central American governments to persuade them not to go along. A State Department briefing paper for U.S. ambassadors in Central America told them that collapse of the Contadora project would be preferable to "a bad agreement," by which it meant an agreement that would leave the Sandinistas in power. It also stressed the long-standing U.S. policy of keeping the Latin Americans divided among themselves. "We need," it said, "to develop an active diplomacy now to head off efforts at Latin solidarity aimed against the United States and our allies." Costa Rica and Honduras yielded to the pressures and refused to sign. Washington was jubilant. Minutes of a National Security Council meeting in November 1984, leaked to the *Washington Post,* recorded the self-congratulations of the members for having sabotaged Contadora.[2]

The Contadora and Support Group nations received international support in December 1986 when UN Secretary General Javier Pérez de Cuellar and OAS Secretary General João Clemente Baena Soares met with them in Rio de Janeiro and decided to meet three times a year to continue discussion of Central American issues and other important hemispheric concerns. This Group of Rio de Janeiro sent representatives to Central America in January 1987 to stress the urgency of acting on the Contadora project. The United States publicly criticized Pérez de Cuellar and Soares for their mission to Central America, a criticism that was rejected with equal publicity by the OAS Permanent Council.

Support also came from twelve European nations which sent delegates to Guatemala City in February to reaffirm their solidarity with the Contadora plan as the most helpful way to regional peace. They condemned U.S. aid for the contras, the British representative declaring that "we don't believe the problems of the area can be resolved by armed force."

Some weeks before this meeting, the Assistant Secretary of State for Inter-American Affairs, Elliott Abrams, and U.S. special envoy Philip Habib met privately with Costa Rica's foreign minister, Rodrigo Madrigal Nieto. Very soon afterward, Costa Rican President Oscar Arias, who had previously been careful to maintain a neutral attitude toward his Nicaraguan neighbors, began to criticize the Managuan regime as a threat to regional peace. On 16 February he presented to the presidents of El Salvador, Guatemala, and Honduras, at a meeting in San José to which President Daniel Ortega had pointedly not been invited, a new peace plan. It incorporated substantial portions of Contadora but added clauses calling for direct negotiations between the Sandinistas and the contras and for new "free" elections.

The implications of the new conditions were clear. In August 1981, Mexico and France had jointly extended recognition to the FDR-FMLN, the political and military arms of the popular movement in El Salvador, as "a belligerent force." This action was an international recognition of their status as a legitimate contender for power in El Salvador. Washington from that time has been trying to establish a symmetry between the contras and the FDR-FMLN, which would mean acceptance of the contras as a legitimate political force with a broad popular base in Nicaragua. In fact, the differences are enormous. The FMLN control a third of El Salvador's national territory, whereas the contras have failed to establish a base in any populated area of the country. The FDR-FMLN rely on almost no external support. The contras are totally dependent on funding openly provided by the U.S. Congress and on major additional U.S. covert aid. The Salvadoran armed forces recognize the broad civilian base of the FMLN and devote a large part of their effort to drying up the sea in which the FMLN swim by depopulating the contested zones of the country. The contras have little or no popular support after six years of fighting.

Equally unacceptable to the Nicaraguan government was the implication in the original Arias plan that the 1984 elections in Nicaragua had not been free, when all international observers had given them high marks, many contrasting them with elections in El Salvador and Guatemala in which a large part of the electorate had been disenfranchised or denied representation.

By this time, however, the Latin American front opposed to Washington's manipulation of Central America had grown so solid that the presidents not only refused to sign but insisted that President Ortega be invited to a renewal of the discussion in May. For that meeting, Arias significantly modified his plan, proposing a dialogue between the Sandinistas and the internal (unarmed) opposition, and for new elections in Nicaragua at the time (in 1990) mandated by the Constitution.

The plan listed a series of measures designed to create conditions for peace in Central America:

1. An amnesty for the rebels in countries in which armed struggle exists.

2. A ceasefire between the armed forces and insurgent groups, and a dialogue between the governments and unarmed internal opposition groups.

3. Full freedom of the press and of political activity within sixty days.

4. Elections for a Central American Parliament in 1988, and national elections as stipulated by each country's constitution.

5. Suspension of military aid from outside the region to insurgent or irregular forces.

6. Prohibition of the use of the territory of any Central American nation for aggression against other states.

7. Creation of an international commission to monitor the accord.

The United States continued intense diplomatic efforts to block the signing of a treaty that formally established the failure of its efforts to isolate Nicaragua from its neighbors. A few hours after Philip Habib had visited him, President Duarte called for additional study and thus postponed a decision in June 1987. But the showdown came the following month in Guatemala when the five presidents affixed their signatures to the document. Duarte was persuaded to join when the provision to deny aid to irregular forces was broadened to include specifically aid from within Central America as well as aid from outside. He had always claimed that Nicaragua was giving major aid to the FMLN.

The night before the signing, President Reagan made a last desperate effort to derail the process. He persuaded Speaker of the House Jim Wright, a Democrat who had consistently opposed aid to the contras, to join him in a new peace plan, actually a rehash of a plan concocted by former Sub-Secretary Tom Enders in 1983. Completely ignoring both the previous peace efforts and the far greater obstacles to peace in El Salvador and Guatemala, it focused on Nicaragua, demanding that it scrap its 1984 elections and hold new elections by 30 September. Simultaneously U.S. administration officials flooded the region in an effort to persuade the Salvadoran and Honduran presidents, the two most dependent on the United States, not to sign any agreement at the Guatemala City meeting. The heavy-handed tactics backfired, however. In an unprecedented declaration of independence, the five presidents agreed to ignore the U.S. document. It was an assertion that Central America was no longer willing to carry the material and moral cost of the U.S.-sustained war of civil strife.

The presidents' revolt against U.S. hegemony was possible because of a conjuncture of events that weakened the Reagan administration. It was the general perception in Latin America and Western Europe, and to a growing extent within the United States, that the Nicaraguan armed forces had inflicted such serious strategic defeats on the contras that not even Reagan could restore their credibility. But the U.S. administration was not ready to give up. The first indication was the resignation of special envoy and troubleshooter Philip Habib who had taken the heretical position of publicly approving the revised Arias plan, which is usually referred to as Esquipulas II to distinguish it from the original Arias proposal. Esquipulas, a national shrine near Guatemala City was the location to which the presidents had been invited for their June meeting. In fact, both the June and July meetings took place, not in Esquipulas, but in Guatemala City.

Superhawk Elliott Abrams, Assistant Secretary of State for Latin America, spearheaded the propaganda offensive. The accord, he said was "more a preliminary agreement than a final peace treaty." It contained "many ambiguities." Instructions went out to State Department officials in Central America to stress U.S. misgivings. Until the Sandinistas had "irreversibly" installed democracy in Nicaragua, the U.S. government would continue to support the contras. Here we have an all-purpose escape hatch, since Washington has to be the judge of democracy and irreversibility.

This response of the U.S. administration to Esquipulas II, however, is important to the extent that it establishes more clearly than ever before what it is that for Washington is not negotiable. The original reason offered for aid to the contras was to compel the Sandinistas to democratize and to stop Nicaragua aiding revolution among its neighbors. Now these same neighbors proclaim that they are ready to work out their relations with it without outside interference. So the U.S. administration is forced to reveal its true objectives: the elimination of the revolutionary government and the reincorporation of Nicaragua into its empire.

Internal politics in the Central American countries played a part in achieving consensus on Esquipulas II. Salvadoran President Duarte had lost most of the slight popular support he had when elected, thanks to his failure to end the war and improve the economy. Pressured by both right and left, he could hope for a measure of domestic and international recognition if the plan worked. In addition, he may have seen the peace proposals as likely to split the more moderate FDR from its more radical FMLN partners. Guatemalan President Cerezo stood mostly to benefit from international approval of his maintenance of Guatemala's relative independence from U.S. regional policy. He had not improved the economic situation and he did not control the military. His only hope for continuance of civilian governments was and is international public opinion. For Arias himself, the benefits were multiple. Continuance of hostile relations with Nicaragua, aggravated by the presence of the contras, is bad for Central American trade which Costa Rica needs. It is also undermining what has long been Costa Rica's glory, the elimination of armed forces. Revelations in the Tower Report and the Iran-Contra hearings of Costa Rican submission to U.S. demands were embarrassing to Arias and to Costa Rica. And for him personally, the international approval of his peace initiative from the outset was a strong incentive to carry it through.

Esquipulas II was given another boost when President Arias himself was awarded the Nobel Peace Prize. Coupled with widespread support expressed by European countries, this added to Washington's problems in trying to scuttle the process. But it did not stop the Reagan administration from continuing to try, concentrating its efforts on presenting the other nations as being in full compliance with the treaty's stipulations while constantly charging Nicaragua with failing to comply. Arias himself was quickly made to feel Washington's displeasure, expressed in the form of strong economic and political retaliatory measures against Costa Rica. They included the suspension of $140 million legislated for Costa Rica for the last six months of 1987, bans and restrictions on Costa Rican exports, and a refusal by the United States for the first time to advocate for Costa Rica with U.S. commercial banks, thereby causing the banks to deny new loans and the rescheduling of existing loans, and also causing holdups of loan agreements with the International Monetary Fund and the World Bank.

In early October, President Reagan formulated a series of new demands: that Nicaragua hold elections well before the 1990 date demanded by the Constitution, which is the date stipulated in Esquipulas II; expulsion of all Soviet and Cuban military advisers and refusal of further military aid from the socialist countries; reduction of the size of the armed forces, release of all "political" prisoners, to include National Guardsmen sentenced for criminal acts; negotiation of a cease-fire with the contras and authorization for their leaders to run for elective office. House Speaker Jim Wright denounced the demands as "ridiculous" and a creation of "the extreme right wing," and Wright withdrew from his short-lived partnership with Reagan. The National Commission for the Protection and Promotion of Human Rights says that some 2,300 former National Guardsmen and counterrevolutionaries are serving sentences for criminal actions. The Permanent Commission on Human Rights, politically close to the internal (legal) opposition, puts the number at over 7,000.

The fact was that Nicaragua from the outset showed its good faith by taking the initiative. It was the first Central American nation to name its Reconciliation Committee, and it named its archcritic, Cardinal Obando y Bravo, as Committee president. At its September meeting this Committee announced the creation of regional commissions, each headed by the local Catholic bishop or his representative and including a representative of the regional government, of the Red Cross, and of the opposition political parties. Other goodwill gestures included the reopening of the opposition newspaper, *La Prensa,* closed in 1986 after the U.S. Congress approved $100 million for the contras, abolition of prior censorship, reopening of Radio Católica (off the air since January 1987), and authorization for Bishop Vega, Monsignor Bismarck Carballo, and an expelled Italian priest to return. Vega refused to return, saying he was more at home with the Nicaraguans in Miami. Bismarck Carballo, however, did return and resumed his work as head of Radio Católica. He applied for, and was granted, a permit to transmit news. The station had been closed for broadcasting news without the authorization required under the State of Emergency.

In addition, the national dialogue between the government and opposition groups, as demanded by Esquipulas II, was initiated in October. Eleven political parties, including several that had boycotted the 1984 elections, were invited, and they named delegates. The rightwing Coordinadora Democrática, dominated by COSEP (the professional organization of big business interests) was also invited to participate, as were trade unions and other groups.

By urging outside powers to stop assistance to guerrilla groups, Esquipulas II challenged both Moscow and Washington to let the region settle its own problems. The United States, however, quickly showed that it was not prepared to abdicate its long-standing claim to dictate in Central America. Instead, it modified its strategy to promote the idea that only Nicaragua was required to make changes, claiming that the other four nations were already fully democratic in their political institutions. It also managed to write the contras into the plan by continuing to channel military aid to them through Honduras while persuading Congress to continue to provide small amounts of "nonlethal" aid. And it encouraged the contras to insist, as a preliminary to a cease-fire, on face-to-face talks with the Nicaraguan government, something Esquipulas II did not require. Also, to make it more difficult for Nicaragua to ease up on the restrictions on freedom of expression imposed by all states in wartime, the United States stepped up the supply of military equipment to the contras. A U.S. State Department spokesman told the Miami Herald that 250,000 pounds of supplies were airdropped in October, almost double the average for each of the preceding thirty months.

Arias tried for a time to out-maneuver Washington. He persuaded President Ortega to accept direct talks with the contras and to suspend a state of emergency, the suspension to take automatic effect when the International Verification Commission created by the Arias peace plan certified that the neighboring countries had taken steps to end use of their territory by the contras and had asked the United States to end aid to the contras. But, because of the opposition of the Honduran army, he was unable to get Honduras to expel the contras, although the peace plan specifically obligated the signatories "to prevent the use of their own territory and to neither render or permit military or logistical support to persons, organizations, or groups attempting to destabilize the governments of the Central American countries." Similarly, he was stymied by the Salvadoran and Guatemalan armies in his efforts to get these countries to enter into meaningful peace talks with their domestic opposition. Once again it was demonstrated that in all three countries the armed forces are the final arbiters of power.

The award of the Nobel Peace Prize to Arias, announced in October, and the overwhelming international jubilation at the choice, constituted a political defeat for Washington. It meant, at least, that Washington was unable to impose its view that the plan must be considered dead if all eleven points were not fully implemented on November 5, the first specified deadline for evaluation. Washington, nevertheless, continued its offensive designed to kill the plan and reinstate its own program for a military solution of Central America's problems. In December, the contras published their conditions for a ceasefire, conditions "drafted by U.S. officials," according to *Newsweek*. They called for an undoing of the social changes made by the revolutionary government: dismantling of agricultural cooperatives, dissolving of the neighborhood associations, suspension of the ra-

tion card system that guarantees minimum supplies of basic foods at controlled prices, an end to all state control of the distribution system, and
suspension of the draft. Another condition was that the government should
recognize that the contras controlled more than half of the national territory, and that the Nicaraguan army should withdraw from this part of the
country. The accompanying map listed as contra-controlled Estelí, Matagalpa, Ocatal, Bluefields, Puerto Cabezas, and many other cities, in none
of which the contras had ever established themselves for a single day. Although President Arias has consistently tried to avoid any appearance of
partiality, he referred to the "intransigence, inflexibility, and intolerance"
of the contras in his Nobel Prize acceptance speech in Oslo, 9 December.
"When you look at the list of conditions and prerequisites," he said, "you
become very pessimistic." Then, pointing to the source of the contras' inflexibility, he appealed to the Reagan administration to support the peace
process by stopping any aid to the contras, including "nonlethal" or "hu-
manitarian."

Not surprisingly, no progress had been made toward a ceasefire in
Nicaragua when the five presidents met in San José, Costa Rica, 15
January 1988, for the next formal evaluation of progress. To verify compliance, the peace plan had established an international verification and
follow-up commission "comprised of the Secretaries General of the Organization of American States and the United Nations or their representatives, as well as the foreign ministers of Central America, of the Contadora Group, and the Support Group." This commission, it specified,
"will have the duties of verifying and following up the compliance with the
commitments undertaken in this document, as well as the support and
facilities given to the mechanisms for reconciliation and verification and
follow-up."

The Verification Commission presented a detailed report, dated 14
January, on the extent to which each of the five countries had and had not
fulfilled its obligations under the accord. The U.S. press ignored this report
almost completely, noting that no country was completely in compliance
while stressing that the commission had been biased in Nicaragua's favor.
Given the composition of the commission, most of whose members represent countries clearly on record as unfriendly to the Nicaraguan revolution,

this interpretation is explicable only on the assumption that the wire services and the media swallowed unquestioningly Washington's propaganda.

In fact, the report is central to the ongoing peace process, and the membership of the committee is such as to place its conclusion beyond challenge. Its opening paragraph sets the tone. It notes "the clear desire of the Central American peoples for peace, their longing for the creation or perfecting of democratic, pluralistic, and participatory governments, which will be the fruit of their will as freely expressed at the polls, and which will ensure the full enjoyment of human rights, economic development, and the overcoming of unjust and obsolete social structures, as well as the legitimate right to decide their own free destinies without outside interference."

It next states clearly what is blocking the peace process. "The strong desire of the Central American peoples for peace, and political, economic, and social democratization is being blocked by a geopolitical fight that does not concern them, and by domineering interests that have nothing to do with their own aspirations."

A later paragraph makes even more specific this general condemnation of outside powers for using the Central Americans as pawns in their conflicts. It is the only mention by name of an outside interfering power. "In spite of the exhortation of the Central American presidents, the government of the United States of America maintains its policy and practice of providing assistance, military in particular, to the irregular forces operating against the government of Nicaragua. The definitive cessation of this assistance continues to be an indispensable requirement for the success of the peace efforts and of this procedure as a whole."

The Committee stressed that "just as the deterioration of the political, economic, and social structure of Central America did not occur suddenly, so peace in the area also cannot be obtained suddenly." It would be untrue to claim success just five months after the signing of the peace agreement, but it would be equally untrue "to deny progress." One unsolved problem, it said, was that it still lacked power to set up mechanisms for on-site inspection, and in consequence it was unable to verify charges by some governments of continuing use of neighboring territory to harass them or support guerrilla movements. It recommended that the five presidents ask the Secretaries General of the United Nations and the Organization of American States to set up mobile verification units in the region. It also recommended that international organizations be asked to help the Verification Commission to examine observance of human rights, democratization, national elections, and elections to the Central American parliament.

Implementation of these recommendations would mean the undoing of the entire U.S. project to prevent by force of arms social change in Central America. A delegation of high Administration officials, including national security adviser, Lt. Gen. Colin L. Powell, and Assistant Secretary of State Elliott Abrams, went to Honduras, El Salvador, Guatemala, and Costa Rica, to tell the presidents they need not expect any more economic aid if the war ended, and the war would end unless they blamed Nicaragua and thus persuaded Congress to vote new aid to the contras.

The blackmail was so blatant that Rep. Tony Coelho (California), House Democratic whip, denounced General Powell for trying to "manipulate the peace process to avoid a settlement." But the presidents of El Salvador, Guatemala, and Honduras had an even more insistent reason to follow Washington's advice. An independent verification committee would expose the fact that none of them had implemented or could implement their commitments, because the armed forces in all three countries would block any such inquiry. In consequence, when they met on 15 January, glossing over the report of the international verification committee, they ruled—over Nicaragua's protest—that the committee had discharged its function and that only the foreign ministers of the five countries would continue to verify the implementation of the peace process.

Buoyed by his success in eliminating the verification commission, President Reagan moved to obtain what he could present as the continuing approval of the U.S. people for his Central American policy, namely, a new Congressional aid package for the contras. In November 1987, he said he would ask for $270 million, but he had made the request more palatable by voting time on 3 February 1988 by cutting it to $43 million, of which only $3.6 million was to be spent on weapons and a further $7 million on electronic devices to assist and protect aircraft ferrying supplies to the contras. The weeks preceding the vote were marked by the most concentrated propaganda effort to date to persuade the public and Congress that Nicaragua continues to be a mortal threat to the security of the United States and that its government had failed to work in good faith to implement Esquipulas II.

Although the Central American presidents had yielded on the verification issue, they remained firm in their insistence that the contras must go. The debate in Congress, in addition, made it clearer than ever before that the Nicaraguan government cannot move further in implementing the peace plan until the armed aggression by the contras ends. By a narrow margin of eight votes the House of Representatives rejected the Reagan aid package in its entirety.

The day-long debate that preceded the vote revealed, however, that most of those who rejected the Reagan proposal share the President's objective of reversing the revolutionary process in Nicaragua even if they do not approve of the means he has been using and wants to continue to use. In other words, the consensus of decision makers in the United States still supports the Miller Doctrine (see page 44) and claims the right to interfere in the internal affairs of the nations of Central America. Given this continuing ambivalence of Congress, it would not be surprising if the Administration found ways to continue funding the contras and also those elements within Nicaragua who stand to lose by social change. The Administration has shown remarkable creativy in bypassing Congressional restrictions, not to mention its shameless readiness to violate both domestic and international law.

The rejection of the Reagan aid package for the contras is, nevertheless, a turning point. Both domestic and international opinion has been alerted as never before to the issues. Latin American opposition to the U.S. claim to hegemony in the hemisphere has been solidified. The U.S. Administration's charges that the Nicaraguan government is totalitarian and non-representative of its people have backfired. It is clearer than ever that this government is more responsive to the wishes of the vast majority of citizens and more protective of their human rights than any of its neighbors.

Other than Nicaragua, Costa Rica is the only Central American country that has taken significant steps to implement the accord, including the closing of a public relations office of the contras in San José. But in El Salvador, Honduras, and Guatemala, violations of human rights have escalated since the signing of the accord in August 1987. A year-end Americas Watch report on El Salvador said the year was marked "by continuation of abuses suffered in the past." The National Union of Salvadoran Workers, El Salvador's major labor group, said in late December that the Duarte government had "Machiavellian plans" to systematically repress the opposition, documenting its charge with eighteen major violations of human rights since the signing of the Arias accord. Also in December, Bishop Gregorio Rosa Chávez, auxiliary of San Salvador, said he had established that one of two prisoners killed in jail had died as a result of torture, and that he was investigating the circumstances of the other killing. The amnesty proclaimed in El Salvador was mainly for the military and the death squads, and it was bitterly but unsuccessfully opposed by human rights groups, labor, and the church. Since 1980, six members of a Human Rights Commission founded in 1978 have been tortured, and eight others have been killed or "disappeared," the most recent in late October 1987.

Guatemala has similarly done nothing to restore the basic rights of its citizens. Those responsible for thousands of murders and disappearances not only go unpunished but are protected by amnesty decrees. The countryside remains militarized. The peasants are impressed into civil patrols and forced to live in the Vietnam-style hamlets. In Honduras, according to Bishop Luis Alfonso Santos of Copán, torture continues to be used, and "there is really no judicial power.... Under the pretext of struggling against communism the most basic civil rights are denied to citizens." In addition, the contra bases in Honduras remain intact. Ramon Custodio, president of the Commission for the Defense of Human Rights in Central America and of the Honduran Human Rights Commission, similarly stated in late October that killings by the security forces were becoming "more blatant," citing the murder of a trade union leader, unarmed young men, and thirty criminals, and adding that "political prisoners are not given the chance to be taken alive." Since 1985, he said, the human rights situation has become worse. "Before, there was talk of disappearances and torture; now, they simply kill." In Guatemala and El Salvador, as well as in Honduras, he concluded, the human rights situation has deteriorated since the accords were signed. "The little hope there is that human rights will improve in the region is steadily decreasing."

Notes

1. *Miami Herald,* 7 December 1986.

2. Mesoamerica, Costa Rica, September 1987.

7.

Building Peace

We cannot even begin to build a more human society in Central America until a way is found to stop the slaughter and engage in a political search for a new equilibrium. That, in turn, cannot happen until the United States abandons its determination to impose its will on these neighbors, in violation alike of international law and the principles it professes. It is, nevertheless, important to develop a vision of what the region might be like, and what might be its relations with the United States, given the opportunity to make its own decisions. Ultimately, only an informed U.S. public opinion can force the country's decision makers to change their present unrealistic and immoral goals. And in making up our minds, we will want to know what will be the implications of change. We will be more inclined to work for it if we can see benefits not only for Central Americans but also for ourselves.

122

Perhaps the most complicated issue is that raised by the commitment in Esquipulas II to free elections in which all the political and social groups will compete on equal terms. Each country is committed to hold such elections at the date specified in its constitution. All five countries are to have elections, but at different dates, between now and 1990.

It is perfectly clear that at least three of the five countries, El Salvador, Guatemala, and Honduras, will find themselves with an overwhelming majority in their legislatures committed to radical change in their social structures. Spokespersons for the popular majorities in those countries have formulated programs that in general terms follow the Nicaraguan model: massive investments in land reform, health, and education, and public controls to ensure that the goods and services generated by the economy are equitably distributed, with the basic needs of all citizens taking precedence over the luxuries of some. Given the history of intransigence of the dominant groups in these countries, such a transfer of power is not going to be easy. Probably no significant progress can be expected unless and until, in addition to the total elimination of foreign military presence in all its forms, a major reduction in the armed forces of these countries is effected under Contadora-type guarantees.

If these preconditions are met, it will be possible for Central America to move rapidly toward a situation in which all its citizens will be able to enjoy modest but adequate living conditions. The region has good land, underutilized supplies of labor, and a geographic location that offers opportunity for many kinds of economic activity, from industry to tourism. The specific directions in which Central America will move, given the fulfillment of the preconditions just set out, cannot be projected in advance. The people of Central America are determined to, and have every right to plot their own future. The Central American parliament proposed in Esquipulas II can serve as a vehicle to enable them to make their own determinations.

Already Central American economists and social scientists are developing scenarios that incorporate some of the possibilities. Many of them are associated with CRIES (Coordinador Regional de Investigaciones Económicas y Sociales: "Regional coordinator of Economic and Social Investigations"). CRIES, in turn, works closely with outside groups such as the

U.S.-based PACCA (Policy Alternatives for the Caribbean and Central America) and the Canadian-based CAPA (Canada Caribbean-Central America Policy Alternatives), two associations of scholars and policy makers.[1]

These scientists start from the assumption that the United States, while reversing its longtime policy of imposing its solutions on Central America, will recognize that it is in its own interest to help create the prosperity without which there can never be stability in the region. They estimate that the major multilateral program of assistance to Central America needed to repair war damage and to begin and sustain the development process will require $2 billion in start-up costs and a further $16 billion between 1987 and 1992. They propose that the United States contribute half, the balance to come from other countries and from such multilateral institutions as the World Bank. The cost to the U.S. taxpayer of military policy in the region is now $9.5 billion a year. The proposed U.S. contribution for peace is $9 billion spread over six years.[2]

Any program of development designed to satisfy the needs of the majority of Central Americans will require reformulation of economic goals. For many reasons, including geography, the United States should continue to be a major economic partner, but it should no longer enjoy a monopoly. Economic and political links should be forged or strengthened with Europe, Canada, non-aligned nations of the developing world, and the socialist countries, with special attention to those Latin American countries to the south whose economies offer many of the goods and services Central America needs. For the foreseeable future, Central America cannot hope to become economically independent. What it can do is to strengthen its position by diversifying its dependence.

CRIES and others have been particularly critical of the Reagan administration's Caribbean Basin Initiative (CBI) on the ground that the incentives it offers actively discourage economic relations between the Central American countries, promoting instead trade with and investment from the United States. They call for greater complementarity between the five countries in production, commerce, and finance, to replace the present practice of competing with each other in external markets and offering the cheapest labor and highest incentives to attract private investment. They also urge closer relations with Panama which has a large transnational service sector, and also more cooperation with the Caribbean countries.

The region's economies at the present time depend on the export of a few primary commodities and light manufactures produced by exploited labor. Instead of depending on a comparative advantage based on the international competition of misery, investment should be redirected toward building internal and regional markets, local processing of raw materials, and promoting the domestic output of grains.

More important than production, however, is the allocation of the benefits. Growth should be seen not as an end in itself but as a means to the satisfaction of basic needs, and subject to that priority, as laying the groundwork for progressive improvement of living levels. Human capital would be mobilized as a principal resource for internal development and it would seek to attract outside resources on the basis of a healthy and educated labor force.[3]

It goes without saying that without generous cooperation by the United States the success of this project is unthinkable. But if one thing is clear, it is that the present U.S. policy of seeking to impose its project by brute force is not working. As the people who have from time immemorial been voiceless and powerless find their voice and recognize their power, it will become progressively less viable. If we seek a world governed by law, a world free from unrest and violence, a world in which democracy is possible, we must change course. And by doing so, we will be returning to our own roots, to the principles on which the United States was founded. Secrecy and deceit will no longer be necessary as instruments of public policy. Instead, we can once more offer an example of cooperation with the dynamic forces that are moving the world toward more human structures that will guarantee to all members of the human race access to food, clothing, shelter, health, education, and dignity.

Notes

1. Richard Fagen, *Forging Peace: The Challenge of Central America*. New York and Oxford (England): Basil Blackwood, 1987, passim.

2. Fagen, op. cit., p. 127; Joshua Cohen and Joel Rogers, *Inequity and Intervention*. Boston: South End Press, 1986, pp. 42-48.

3. Fagen, op. cit., passim.

Index